Greenhouse Gardening

Step by Step to Growing Success

Jonathan Edwards

First Published in 1988 by
The Crowood Press Ltd
Ramsbury, Marlborough
Wiltshire SN8 2HR

www.crowood.com

Revised edition 1996
This impression 2004

British Library Cataloguing in Publication Data
A catalogue record for this publication is available from the British Library.

ISBN 1 85223 976 X

Picture Credits
All photographs by Dave Pike except for the step-by-step pictures on the following pages by Dr EJM Evesham: 31, 32, 34, 35, 36, 37, 66, 67, 84, 92, 93 and 97.

All colour artwork by Claire Upsdale-Jones.

Dedication
To Mum and Dad.

Typeset and designed by
D & N Publishing
Ramsbury, Marlborough
Wiltshire SN8 2HR

Typeface used: Plantin.

Imagesetting by Dorwyn Ltd, Chichester.

Printed and bound in Malaysia by Times Offset (M) Sdn. Bhd.

Contents

Introduction

Whatever your experience or expertise, a greenhouse offers the chance to extend your gardening activities. You can use it to help save money by raising bedding and vegetables from seed every year, as well as propagating other plants to fill garden beds and borders. If you can install a reliable source of heat, there's an opportunity to get off to an earlier start and grow crops that require a long growing season. In colder climes, a heated greenhouse enables you to grow crops that would not thrive outside, and in a milder climate the options are almost limitless. For many gardeners, though, a greenhouse is a retreat where they can escape the worst of the weather and still carry on with their favourite hobby.

No matter what your reasons are for buying a greenhouse, you will get a lot more from it if you plan carefully and keep a watchful eye on the plants you are growing. This book will help you choose the right greenhouse and enjoy growing success for years to come.

Mini-rose 'Sunblaze'.

CHAPTER 1

Choosing a Greenhouse

Greenhouses are better value today than ever before: a standard 8 × 6ft (2.5 × 1.8m) aluminium model is available at low prices everywhere from the garden centre and superstores to the high street supermarket. Having said that, a word of caution. If your choice is governed by price alone you will almost certainly live to regret it. Do not buy in haste.

If this purchase is your first greenhouse then you may well find the specifications from competing manufacturers bewildering. You need to make a checklist of your own requirements and see how each model on offer measures up to it.

WHAT SHAPE IS MOST SUITABLE?

Greenhouses are available in a range of shapes (*see* box). As a first-time buyer of a greenhouse, the shape might not seem all that important apart from the obvious aesthetic consideration. However, the shape you choose should be determined by the type of crops you intend to grow. For instance, if you want to grow bulky crops, such as tomatoes or cucumbers that need to be trained up and along supporting wires, or taller flower crops such as chrysanthemums, then a traditional straight-sided greenhouse with an eave height of at least 5ft (1.5m) would be a good choice. You can still grow such crops in greenhouses with sloping sides, but the growing space will be significantly reduced. High eaves and straight sides will also allow you to put up more staging thereby increasing the available growing space even further. If, on the other hand, you want to extend this rather limited growing season and utilize your greenhouse throughout the year, then a better choice would be a model

---

GREENHOUSE SHAPES

TRADITIONAL STRAIGHT SIDES

❀ Widely available
❀ Inexpensive
❀ High eaves – ideal for growing tomatoes and other tall crops
❀ Can accommodate large area of bench space

SLOPING SIDES

❀ Fairly widely available
❀ Admits more light than straight-sided model
❀ Cheaper to heat because less volume

CURVED EAVES

❀ Attractive
❀ Admits more light than straight-sided model

POLYGONAL

❀ Attractive

LEAN-TO

❀ Admits more light than straight-sided
❀ Takes less space
❀ Good headroom

---

with sloping sides, because they allow greater light transmission during the critical winter months. Rather smart glass domes are now available and are ideal for the low-growing winter crops like lettuce or displays of prize alpines on staging.

The height of the greenhouse ridge should be determined by your height. Surprisingly, ridge heights vary considerably, so if you are over 5ft 10in (1.78m) then make sure the model you buy has a ridge height of at least 7ft (2.1m). You can increase

A round aluminium greenhouse.

both the eaves and ridge height of a greenhouse by setting the greenhouse on a low wall – up to two courses of bricks high. However, this will make access more difficult with a wheelbarrow.

WHAT SIZE SHOULD I BUY?

Size is determined by finances and available space. If you are a beginner taking your first tentative steps into greenhouse gardening then choose a wide, short greenhouse that can be added to as needs and ready cash allow. Check, though, that the model you buy can be added to using extension modules.

A well-managed 6 × 8ft (1.8 × 2.5m) greenhouse will offer enough growing space for most gardeners.

It is also worth investing in a cold frame, say 3 × 4ft (90 × 122cm) to provide additional temporary space in mid- and late spring when the greenhouse is full to overflowing.

If you intend doing some serious greenhouse gardening, then buy the biggest you can afford – it's even worth doing without some of the accessories for a couple of seasons to get that extra couple of feet of growing space.

Where garden space is the limiting factor, then a lean-to model is worth considering, but do site it against a sunny wall unless you intend growing ferns.

Lean-tos

These are designed to be attached to the side of a house or garage. Usually shaped like half a standard greenhouse they take less room and can be more convenient than a free-standing model. The house wall also helps protect it, so lean-tos cost less to heat. If you don't intend heating your greenhouse, a lean-to will provide more frost protection in winter too.

An aluminium lean-to.

Lean-tos can be attached to any wall, provided the mortar is sound and the ridge of the greenhouse will fit under the eaves of the house. If fitted over the back door of the house and will be used as a thoroughfare, it's worth putting safety glass in the roof sections. Seal the greenhouse to the house wall using waterproof flashing to prevent leaks that may lead to damp penetrating the house wall.

It is tempting to put up a lean-to on a south-facing wall, but it will be difficult to keep cool enough in winter: an east- or west-facing site would be easier to manage.

IS GLASS BETTER THAN PLASTIC?

Most greenhouses are glazed with 24in (61cm) square panes of horticultural glass (3mm thick). This type of glass is cheap and widely available, so easy to get hold of if you need to replace one or two panes. A few greenhouses are glazed with much larger sheets of glass (often called Dutch lights). Although they let in more light and are easier to clean, they are more difficult to handle and cost more to replace.

Plastic is a recent innovation that hasn't really caught on amongst the gardening fraternity. Although a pretty conservative crowd, gardeners will soon take up anything that has significant

The base of the greenhouse is extremely important, serving both to level the greenhouse and to anchor it against wind.

BUYING CHECKLIST

It is very difficult to assess a greenhouse from a catalogue picture. It is far better to examine an assembled model set up at a retail outlet or at a gardening show. Here's what to check for:

ALUMINIUM-FRAMED MODEL

❋ Make sure sections are strong and are well braced to make them rigid. Look for a greenhouse with at least one wind brace on each side and end; on windy sites opt for a model with braces on the roof too.
❋ Check the corners to make sure they fit together without gaps. Special corner brackets are best but tend to be available only on larger models.
❋ Check that the glazing strip of rubber that cushions the glass panels is in good condition.
❋ Check that glazing bars are grooved to hold clips for attaching insulation and shading materials.

WOODEN-FRAMED MODEL

❋ Make sure all joints are well fitting.
❋ Check that all timber is straight and true with no warps or knots.
❋ Check that pressure-treated softwood has not been cut after treatment (thereby breaching the protection).
❋ Check that all fittings are made from brass or galvanized steel.
❋ Check that glass fits snugly – especially at ridge ends and the base ends.

WITH ALL GREENHOUSES

❋ Check the door fits snugly to the frame leaving no gaps and does not distort when opened.
❋ Make sure it opens easily and is wide and high enough for you and any loads you wish to take in and out.
❋ Check that there is sufficient ventilation included in the basic model price: at least two roof and two side vents in a 6 × 8ft (1.8 × 2.5m) greenhouse.
❋ Check that the price you are quoted includes the base. Make sure the base anchors the greenhouse right round the base of the frame, so that it does not bend or distort in windy conditions.
❋ Get a written quote for any optional extras that you need before buying.

advantages over the competition. So how do these two materials compare?

Well they are pretty equal as regards light transmission, though plastic allows more infra-red light to pass in which warms the greenhouse quickly, but, conversely, lets it out just as fast and so cools down more rapidly, too. Plastic is lighter and needs smaller and fewer supporting bars. It can be curved round to make the heating area smaller without reducing the growing area and is, of course, a lot cheaper than glass. But it does attract dirt by static electricity, is degraded by sunlight so that it becomes brittle and worst of all needs replacing every few years. Even when new, it is prone to splitting or puncturing by careless hands.

The double-skinned, box-section polycarbonate sheeting, on the other hand, is a very strong plastic alternative. It is a good insulator because it traps a layer of air between the two skins, but is very expensive compared to glass so only a worthwhile option if your greenhouse is at risk from vandals such as near a public footpath or isolated on an allotment, for example.

Rigid UPVC is another non-glass option worth considering. It's cheaper than polycarbonate, but it scratches more easily and condensation can be a problem, especially if you are growing winter crops.

If you have young children, it is worth considering having the bottom half and the door of the greenhouse glazed with safety glass. If your children are older the roof may need protecting too! Safety glass is offered as an optional extra by some manufacturers (at an additional cost). Although tougher than horticultural glass, it will still break, but shatters into tiny cubes rather like a car windscreen, so there is no chance of injury from shards of broken glass. A slightly cheaper alternative is special sticky-backed film that can be applied to the inside of ordinary glass. This simply holds the glass in place if accidentally broken.

WHICH HAS MORE TO OFFER: WOOD OR ALUMINIUM?

Aluminium is the most common material used for the greenhouse structure these days. It does not deteriorate with time and so is practically maintenance free. The extruded framework makes the aluminium greenhouse strong while still remaining lightweight. It is relatively cheap when compared to its wooden counterparts and is easy to glaze – although aluminium structures can be complicated to put together if you choose a cheap self-assembly model.

Unfortunately, since it is a metal, aluminium is a poor insulator and tends to conduct expensive heat outside, which can be a problem during early spring. This rapid cooling results in condensation forming on the inside of the greenhouse's frame and glass that encourages disease problems. However, condensation can, to some extent, be eliminated by insulating the structure.

Greenhouses made from softwood are competitively priced and look attractive in the garden setting. The softwood structure does, though, have one significant disadvantage in that it is prone to rotting and needs treating regularly with a wood preservative. This is not only a chore but can be a hazardous occupation, particularly on the wider

A greenhouse with a three-sided wooden bottom section.

A wooden-framed greenhouse, but with the bottom section replaced with glass.

span models. However, with the advent of pressure-treated timber and the introduction of plant-safe preservatives these disadvantages are reduced. Wood also insulates and so is cheaper to heat.

If well made, a wooden structure is flexible enough to support a range of shelves and wires without extra strengthening. Pins can be pushed into the wood allowing quick and easy partitioning with plastic sheeting or the straightforward erection of insulation and shading. Aluminium-framed greenhouses need complex and often expensive clips to achieve the same result.

Cedar is expensive. If you can afford it, though, buy it. It's not too costly to heat, is a good insulator and doesn't suffer from the dreaded condensation. Since cedar is inherently rot resistant it needs little maintenance. A preservation treatment every few years will keep it looking in tip-top condition.

HOW MUCH VENTILATION DO I NEED?

To keep a greenhouse cool in summer it is essential to have sufficient ventilation. Unfortunately, most 'standard' models are not supplied with adequate ventilation, so you will need to pay extra for more to be added. To get a good flow of air through the greenhouse, and as a bare minimum, aim to have ventilation in both the roof and low down at the side. In a very small greenhouse, leaving the door slightly ajar could be used to substitute for a side vent.

In a 6 × 8ft (1.8 × 2.5m) greenhouse ask for at least one roof vent (preferably two) and two side vents. For larger models use the following formula to work out how much ventilation you need. Ideally the open area of the vents should be around one-sixth of the floor area.

Calculate the open area of a hinged vent by multiplying the length of the vent by the amount it opens (length of the stay), plus the width of the vent times the amount it opens. For instance, a 24 × 24in (61 × 61cm) vent on a 9in (23cm) stay will have a maximum open area of 24in (length) × 9in (stay) + 24in (width) × 9in (stay) = 432 sq in (3 sq ft); 2,786 sq cm (0.28 sq m).

Calculate the open area of a louvre vent by simply multiplying the height by the width. For example, a 24 × 24in (61 × 61cm) vent would have a maximum open area of 24in (length) × 24in (width) = 576 sq in (4 sq ft); 3,715 sq cm (0.37 sq m). Therefore, a 10ft × 12ft (3 × 3.6m) greenhouse – floor area 120sq ft (11 sq m) would need 20 sq ft

Petunias can be raised from seed in early spring.

(1.9 sq m) of ventilation open area. This could be supplied by three louvre vents and three roof vents in this example.

Standard hinged, louvred or sliding vents all work adequately. On the side of a greenhouse, however, hinged vents can be a safety hazard. Louvres are draughty in winter and sliding vents have an annoying habit of getting stuck. Aim to have vents on both sides of the greenhouse so that at least one can be opened on the leeward side on windy days.

POLYTHENE TUNNELS

You can now get polythene tunnels suitable for garden use. Several manufacturers offer models from 8ft (2.5m) wide and 10ft (3m) long. They are all similar in design: based on a framework of tubular hoops covered in a polythene sheet. Features to look for:

❀ Polythene is available in several thicknesses: choose at least 720 gauge.
❀ Polythene that has been given an anti-fog coating to stop condensation building up on the inside.
❀ Thermal polythene which retains more heat.
❀ Anti hot-spot tape that protects the polythene during hot weather by insulating it from the frame – you will need sufficient to cover the outer edges of every hoop.
❀ Wooden-framed doors prevent draughts and are easier to use than simple polythene flaps.
❀ If you want to grow taller crops such as tomatoes, opt for a tunnel with straightened sides.
❀ Some models are available with netting sides to keep them cooler in the summer months. In winter, polythene flaps can be rolled down to prevent heat loss.

WHAT ABOUT ACCESS?

Both sliding and hinged doors are available. Sliding doors take less space and can be easily secured in a partially opened position for added ventilation. However, the runners are likely to become clogged and the nylon wheels do sometimes need replacing. Hinged doors need little maintenance apart from a little oil now and again, but they can restrict access, particularly if the door opens inwards. With all doors, though, make sure they are tall enough for you to go in and out without bumping your head and ideally, wide enough to get in and out of the greenhouse with a wheelbarrow otherwise the movement of materials will be a laborious task of carrying to and fro.

ARE THERE ANY HIDDEN EXTRAS?

There are a few manufacturers who are inclined to make essential equipment like vents and greenhouse bases an addition to the basic price. Delivery charges and erection costs can, in some cases, inflate the price out of all recognition.

Check carefully as to what is included in the price before you buy, and obtain a written estimate for the basic price and all extras involved. The best advice of all, though, is to shop around.

Even a small greenhouse can offer the gardener the opportunity to grow an abundance of colourful plants.

CHAPTER 2

Siting a Greenhouse

It doesn't matter how good your greenhouse is or how green your fingers, if your greenhouse is sited in the wrong place (for instance, under overhanging trees) results will be disappointing.

LIGHT

Good light is essential – preferably on an open site well away from fences, buildings and overhanging greenery. If the available light is reduced, then the crop yields will be diminished. Furthermore, in autumn deciduous trees create an additional problem with falling leaves blocking the gutters and drainpipes. Trees also harbour pests and diseases or even spatter your house with a sticky exudate that is soon colonized by algae and moulds.

SHELTER

Although the best light may well be on top of a nearby mountain or hill this is probably the last place you want to site your greenhouse. The exposure, if not destructive, would certainly curtail crop yields and increase heating costs considerably! In effect a balance is needed: away from shade, but sheltered from the worst weather.

FROST POCKETS

Frost pockets can usually be found lurking behind walls or dense evergreen hedges at the bottom of a slope. They are in effect trapped cold air that has run down the slope and been caught by the solid barrier. Don't erect your greenhouse in such a position.

MAINS SERVICES

Supplying water and electricity services to a greenhouse can add considerably to its initial cost. Although desirable, it is not essential to have either. However, it is worth noting that a greenhouse without these services will have limited use. After all, the easier a job the far more likely it is to get done.

If you want these services then they should be a prime consideration when you are deciding on a site since the further a greenhouse is from the mains supply the more costly the installation.

ACCESS

Just as a new town needs to have good road links to prosper, so a new greenhouse needs weather-proof pathways and be conveniently sited. If it is at the bottom of the garden at the end of a long, narrow, muddy path then it will, at best, become a fair-weather hobby.

Best of all, site your greenhouse a few yards from the back door with a clean, even paved access path to it and right around it.

ORIENTATION

Much confusing advice is available about which way to point a greenhouse for the best results. For general-purpose growing the apex of the greenhouse should run north–south, but if you intend cultivating winter crops that need a lot of light then it is better to position it with the apex running east–west. This argument, though, tends to be rather academic since most small gardens do not provide enough space to afford the luxury of choosing direction. The

---

PUTTING UP AN ALUMINIUM GREENHOUSE STEP-BY-STEP

An aluminium greenhouse is made from a surprising number of components. Before you set about trying to put the structure together, it is worth checking them off against the delivery note supplied by the manufacturer. This will not only make sure you have all the bits you need, but will help you to familiarize yourself with the different components.

1. Check that all the 'pre-drilled' holes have been completed and are in the right place.
2. Check aluminium bars are not twisted or damaged.
3. Lightly oil bolts before you start to prevent the nuts sticking.
4. If your greenhouse is supplied with a base, construct this section first making sure each corner is perfectly square (see 'Foundations' opposite).
5. In an open space (e.g. a lawn) assemble each side and end and then both roof sections. Then take each section to the prepared site.
6. Bolt together the various sections according to the manufacturer's instructions. It's worth having

a drill handy just in case a pre-drilled hole isn't in the right place or hasn't been finished properly.
7. Tighten bolts evenly over the greenhouse until it is firm and rigid.
8. Anchor the frame to the base or where no base is being used, concrete in ground anchors according to the manufacturer's instructions.
9. Assemble the door and vents, then attach them to the frame.
10. Glaze the frame from the bottom up on a calm dry day to reduce the risk of breakages.

PUTTING UP A WOODEN GREENHOUSE

This is relatively simple since the sections come ready-assembled. All you need to do is lay the base as for an aluminium greenhouse, then bolt together the sides and ends, fit the ridge bar and roof spars or roof sections and glaze the structure. Some models even come ready glazed.

---

difference it makes is rather marginal anyway, except with a particularly long, narrow greenhouse.

FOUNDATIONS

Laying good foundations makes greenhouse construction a simple job. Many models are available with ready-made bases (sometimes as an optional extra) that consist of pre-cast concrete kerbstones which fit accurately together to form a rectangle. These usually require setting in the ground to a depth of a couple of inches or so. Check that the corners are exactly square using a 3, 4, 5, triangle before firming in the soil. (A triangle of sides 3, 4, and 5 units (inches, metres, etc.) gives an accurate 90-

degree angle.) Also, on exposed sites, further anchorage may be necessary, so consult your dealer.

GLAZING

Always glaze your greenhouse after erection. Many models come with glass cut to size and ready to be slotted into position, but others need glazing. Use horticultural quality glass (3mm or 24oz panes).

On exposed sites, further anchorage may be necessary.

DIY FOUNDATIONS

You can make your own foundations for a greenhouse by digging a trench 8in (20cm) deep and wide, and filling it with concrete. In addition, you could raise the greenhouse slightly by laying one or two courses of bricks on the concrete to match the dimensions of the greenhouse. More than this will make access to the greenhouse difficult.

PUTTING UP A POLYTHENE TUNNEL STEP-BY-STEP

This is quite different from putting up a greenhouse and probably less fiddly, although you will need at least two people (preferably four) when putting on the polythene sheet.

1. Before you start, check through the delivery note to make sure you have all the parts.
2. Mark out and level the site, clear weeds and any other debris.
3. Position pairs of foundation tubes (short pieces of metal tubing that hold the ends of the hoops) so that the sides of the tunnel are straight and the ends at right angles. They will need hammering into firm earth for small tunnels and setting in concrete for larger tunnels.
4. Put together the hoops and slot into the foundation tubes, then fit the corner braces. Tighten all bolts so the frame is rigid.
5. Dig out a trench right round the tunnel (apart from the doorway) to bury the ends of the polythene sheet. A trench 6in (15cm) wide and 6–10in (15–25cm) deep should be sufficient.
6. Assemble the door frame and attach to the end hoop, making sure it is square so the doors fit snugly.
7. Wipe the hoops then put on anti hot-spot tape to all outside edges that would come into contact with the polythene.
8. On a warm, calm day pull the polythene sheet over the frame. Bury one side in the trench already excavated and stretch the sheet evenly over the hoops. The polythene must be kept taught while it is buried in the trench running along the other side. The warmer the day the tighter the polythene fit.
9. Pleat the ends neatly so that they can be attached to the door frame using battens – again pull the polythene as taught as you possibly can before hammering on the battens. Trim any surplus polythene from around the door frame and fit the door.
10. Pull the polythene taught at each end by burying it in the prepared trenches.

Aluminium greenhouses are usually easy to glaze using plastic or rubber bedding strips set in the glazing bars. All you need to do is position the glass and snap in a few glazing clips and the job is done. Wooden structures can be more of a problem, involving the traditional and rather messy business of setting glass on putty and holding with glazing sprigs.

With all types of glazing where panes overlap, start at the bottom and work upwards, otherwise the overlaps won't shed water, but collect it!

Using a 3, 4, 5 triangle to check that the corners of the base are exactly square.

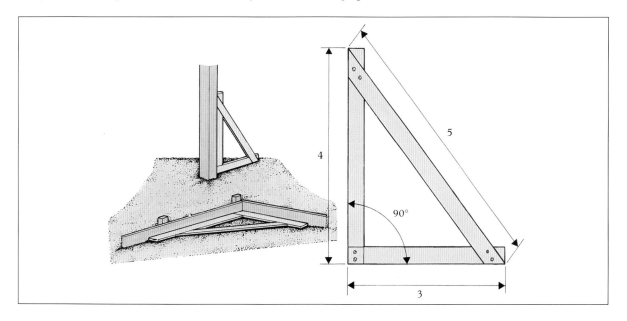

CHAPTER 3

Greenhouse Equipment

HEATING

It is surprising that so few gardeners heat their greenhouses. If you don't provide some form of heat, your growing season will be mid-spring to mid-autumn (several weeks shorter in the north) and the range of crops will also be reduced. The three main reasons often quoted why gardeners are put off heating their greenhouse are that it costs a fortune, heaters need constant supervision and there isn't anything to grow in winter anyway. None of these arguments are true if you take care to select the right heater for your situation and choose the right crops to grow. First of all, make sure your greenhouse is in a fit state to be heated. That is, it is not exposed to the prevailing winds and is fairly air-tight once the vents and doors are closed. Then cut down the volume of air to be heated to the minimum, by partitioning off an area using insulating bubble polythene. Select a heater with a thermostatic control so that it will turn on and off automatically to keep the greenhouse at the correct temperature. Remember an extra 9°F (5°C) can almost double the heating costs.

If you can keep your greenhouse frost free, you'll be able to overwinter tender perennials such as geraniums and fuchsias as well as overwinter early bedding such as antirrhinums. By maintaining a temperature of 45°F (7°C), however, you would be able to grow a wide range of crops all year round.

Heating a Lean-to Greenhouse

You may be able to heat a lean-to greenhouse by extending your household central heating system. By fitting an independent thermostat on radiators in the lean-to you will be able to keep the greenhouse at the right temperature.

CHOOSING THE RIGHT HEATER

These days, you have the choice between electric fan heaters, bottled gas heaters, natural gas heaters or paraffin heaters. There are solid fuel heaters too,

Small paraffin heaters are ideal for the amateur greenhouse.

but they are not really a viable option for a small greenhouse. The different types of heaters have distinct advantages and disadvantages so consider the following before you choose:

Electric

Pros
❀ Clean and small.
❀ Thermostatically controlled so will operate automatically.
❀ Have a fan that moves the air around and keeps the air temperature even throughout the greenhouse.

Cons
❀ Expensive to install if you don't have a mains supply to your greenhouse already.

Paraffin

Pros
❀ Cheap to buy.
❀ No installation costs.

Cons
❀ Needs constant monitoring to maintain correct temperature.

HOW TO AVOID BIG HEATING BILLS

❀ Don't heat your greenhouse to a higher temperature than you need.
❀ Keep the volume of air being heated to a minimum by sectioning off part of your greenhouse. If that section is in the middle of the greenhouse or at least not on the side of prevailing wind, you will reduce your bills further.
❀ Insulate the area being heated. Bubble polythene insulation material can be recouped in one season if you live in a cold area or heat your greenhouse to 45°F (7°C).
❀ Draught-proof your greenhouse.
❀ Start heating after the coldest weather is over by avoiding early sowings.
❀ Install soil-warming cables or buy a heated propagator to avoid heating your greenhouse at all.

❀ Needs filling regularly with fuel.
❀ Produces water vapour that may encourage diseases.
❀ Greenhouse needs ventilating.

Bottled Propane Gas

Pros
❀ Clean.
❀ Thermostatically controlled so will operate automatically.

Cons
❀ Expensive to buy.
❀ Produces water vapour that may encourage diseases.
❀ Greenhouse needs ventilating.

Natural Gas

Pros
❀ Clean and small.
❀ Thermostatically controlled so will operate automatically.

Cons
❀ Can be expensive to install if you do not have a mains gas supply to your greenhouse already in place.
❀ Produces water vapour that may encourage diseases.
❀ Greenhouse needs ventilating.

Safety First

Always stand your heater on a surface that is firm and level where it cannot be accidentally knocked over.
❀ Always keep the area around a heater clear, especially of flammable materials such as bubble polythene.
❀ Always keep the door shut and preferably locked as well to keep children out of a heated greenhouse.
❀ Always use an RCD with an electric heater.
❀ Always use premium grade paraffin.
❀ Always turn off a paraffin heater before moving it.

Soil-warming cables are easy to install in a frame or greenhouse border.

Soil-heating Cables

Heating the entire greenhouse for the sake of a few overwintering plants doesn't make economic sense. It is far better to make or buy a smaller frame and fit it out with bottom heat. Soil-warming cables in

---

MAKING A PROPAGATING FRAME STEP-BY-STEP

1. Construct a sturdy box at least 10in (25cm) deep and line it with polystyrene blocks wrapped in polythene.
2. Even out a 1in (2.5cm) layer of sand in the bottom of the box.
3. Starting a couple of inches inside one corner, space the heating cables evenly over the surface of the sand in a snaking pattern. You will need to allow 85 watts per square yard in a heated greenhouse and 125 watts per square yard in an unheated greenhouse.
4. Cover the cable in 2in (5cm) of sand.
5. Cover this layer with a 4–6in (10–15cm) layer of compost if you want to root cuttings.

---

a small frame can maintain a frost-free temperature for just one or two units each day even during the coldest months. If you are using Economy 7 power then this cost will be very low indeed.

Soil-warming cables are available in several different lengths. Which one you choose will depend on the area you want to heat and the minimum temperature you want to achieve.

For instance, for a greenhouse border you would need to allow about 50 watts per square yard – so a 150 watt 40ft (18m) cable would be sufficient to heat one side of a 6 × 8ft (1.8 × 2.5m) greenhouse. By insulating the soil area with polystyrene blocks wrapped in polythene (for protection) you can keep heating costs to a minimum; make sure there is at least 2in (5cm) of soil between the cable and insulation.

INSULATION

The value of fitting insulation will entirely depend on the location of your greenhouse and the crops you intend growing. For instance,

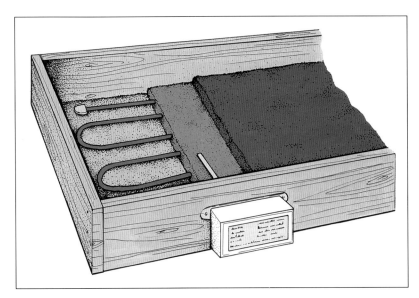

A rod thermostat should be fitted at right angles to the direction of the soil-warming cable loops.

if you are on an exposed spot in the north of Britain and you want to grow early tomatoes, then the money spent on even the most expensive insulation would be recouped in a matter of weeks. But if you are just keeping the frost out in a sheltered corner in the south then it may take you a lifetime to get your money's worth. On average, though, you can expect a saving of up to 45 per cent on the cost of heating a 6 × 8ft (1.8 × 2.5m) greenhouse.

When fitting your insulation make sure the vents are left free of obstruction. Where combustible fuels are being used you will need air movement all winter and, even with electricity, ventilation is essential on those bright spring days when the greenhouse heats up so rapidly.

SHADING

There are many sun-loving plants the beginner can grow that will lap up the all too brief spells of sunshine in the British climate. There may be only two or three months in an average year when shading is really necessary; the rest of the time temperature can be controlled by damping down and careful ventilation.

A beginner can avoid a lot of the need for shading by giving a little thought to the layout of a greenhouse; put sun-loving plants like tomatoes on the south side and the rest on the north side where they will thrive in the shade of their taller neighbours.

External slatted blinds have the advantage that they can be adjusted to suit the conditions from week to week (above right).

A proprietary whitewash applied directly to the glass is a cheaper and easier option (right).

Still, this won't be enough during the hottest months, particularly if it's a scorching summer. The amount of shading you need, therefore, is dependent on the types of plants you grow. But there are also other factors to consider, including where you live; not just how far north, but at what altitude, as well as the situation and condition of your greenhouse. If it's in the shadow of something or has dirty glass then less shading will be required.

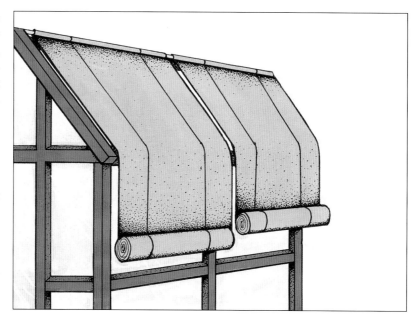

THERMOMETERS

There is a range of thermometers available that are suitable for use in the greenhouse. The best type is the max/min thermometer because it not only allows you to read the temperature when you are in the greenhouse but records what the highest and lowest temperatures were since you last reset it. This means you can check how efficiently your greenhouse heater is working at night and whether the automatic vents are keeping the greenhouse cool enough during the day.

It is essential that a thermometer is positioned correctly if the readings are to mean anything. A thermometer should not be allowed to be exposed to direct sun (reading too high) or placed against the glass (reading too low). For most accurate readings construct a small white-washed, well-ventilated box that can be set amongst the crop being grown, but kept at least 6in (15cm) off the ground.

Choosing Shading

There are basically four types of shading: netting; roller blinds; whitewash; and slatted blinds. Any type of shading attached to the inside of the greenhouse will not keep the greenhouse cool as the sun's rays turn to heat energy on contact with the blind, and this energy is trapped in the greenhouse by the glass – the 'greenhouse effect'. To keep a greenhouse cool as well as shaded it is necessary either to attach materials to the outside of the greenhouse or to apply a whitewash to the glass.

Louvre vents provide good air flow when open, but can be draughty when closed.

The cheapest and easiest option is to use a white-wash shading product that can be applied each spring and removed in the autumn.

VENTILATION

To keep the greenhouse temperature at an optimum level during the spring and summer it is necessary to have some form of ventilation. Even during frosty mornings in spring, sunlight energy spears its way into the greenhouse where it turns to heat energy on coming into contact with soil or staging. This lower frequency heat energy is then unable to escape from the greenhouse, rapidly increasing the temperature of the soil and air.

There are a range of ventilators available to the greenhouse gardener of which the hinged roof vent is probably the most common and found in many of the cheaper greenhouses. Alternatively, some manufacturers offer hinged side-vents, but to get a good through draught of air you'll need both types and preferably more than one of each. Side-mounted hinge vents can be a safety hazard with children, so the flush louvre vents might be more practical. Louvre vents can also give better air circulation than the hinged type, but are less draughtproof when closed.

Sliding vents are available on some models of greenhouse and work wonderfully until a dastardly piece of grit or sticky lump of mud gets lodged in the runner.

Automatic vent openers are a good investment, especially for the busy gardener.

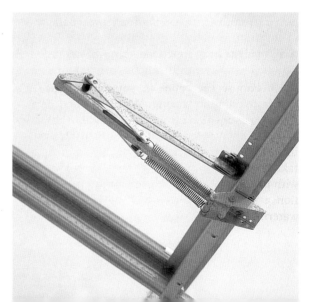

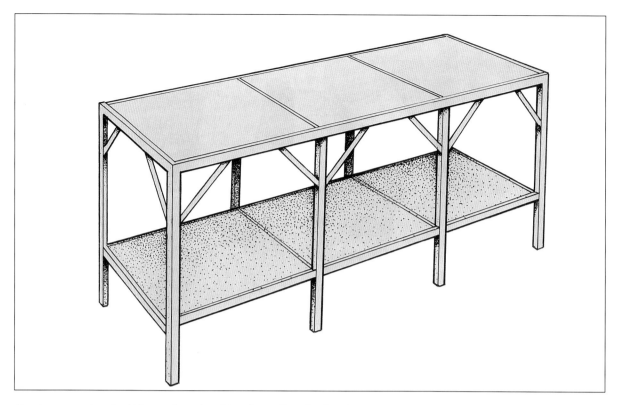

Bench-type staging should be sturdy and positioned on a firm, level surface.

Opening and closing vents becomes a real bore after just a few days and so some form of automatic vent opener is a worthwhile investment. There is a good variety of makes available but they all operate on the same principle: the heat from the sun causes wax that is contained in a cylinder to expand. This forces a piston out which, via some form of adjustable lever system, opens the vent. When the wax cools it contracts allowing the piston to be pushed into the cylinder causing the vent to close.

STAGING

To maximise the room in your greenhouse it's worth investing in staging. Whether wood or aluminium, purpose-built or home-made, it must be strong. Although many of the rigours to which staging is subjected are lightweight, like potting and taking cuttings, in the spring it will be stacked high with plants and heavy with seedtrays – not to mention a propagator and maybe even an automatic watering system.

All staging needs a firm footing to avoid disaster. Make sure the back legs are set solid in the outside wall foundations of the greenhouse and the front on the central path base. If you are making staging remember to get the height exactly right – a few inches too high or too low will soon give you backache when potting or taking cuttings, for example.

Maintenance-free aluminium staging is becoming more popular these days and comes in many shapes and sizes, makes and styles. Some are available with trays that can be reversed to make a flat standing surface. They can also be removed for easy plant handling. Other forms of staging are designed to fold away when not in use – very useful in spring when staging is overflowing with seedlings. Shelving is also a useful addition to the greenhouse to increase growing space.

PROPAGATORS

To a gardener a propagator is nearly as good as money in the bank. It makes it possible to sow seeds in the depths of winter with the minimum of

needed to germinate some of the more exotic species of plants.

The added flexibility a simple propagator gives the greenhouse gardener should also not be overlooked – helping bring on slow germinating subjects as well as enabling the more forgetful of us to sow seed a little later than normally recommended.

The simplest form of propagator is basically a seedtray with a heating pad in its base – the better ones come supplied with a clear plastic lid with adjustable ventilation holes. This is perfectly adequate for germinating the majority of seed offered and is particularly useful if used in conjunction with the

fuss and at little cost. In addition, a propagator increases the range of plants you are able to grow by providing the high temperature environment

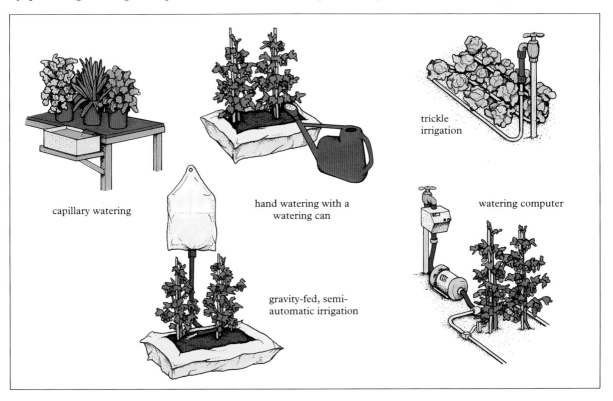

capillary watering

hand watering with a watering can

trickle irrigation

gravity-fed, semi-automatic irrigation

watering computer

There are various types of watering system available.

quarter-size trays that fit snugly inside. You can then sow four different seeds at once without having to worry about their varying rates of germination. Apart from its small size, the main drawback of this type of propagator is the lack of temperature control. Although the heating pad gives out a consistent heat, the actual temperature achieved will fluctuate according to the surrounding environmental temperature.

The versatile thermostatically regulated propagators cost more, but the extra control they afford over the environment makes successful seed germination a little less hit and miss. They tend to be larger too.

Propagators are also ideal for rooting cuttings – offering a constant bottom heat to encourage rooting while keeping the atmosphere humid, so preventing the leafy tops from flagging.

If you intend to overwinter plants in a propagator and thus save on greenhouse heating bills then consider buying one with a high top. This will enable you to save a wider range of tender perennials.

If you don't have an electricity supply in your greenhouse you could consider buying a paraffin-heated propagator. This is basically a small paraffin heater that stands underneath a galvanised table. This heats up, keeping the seedlings standing on top in a cosy environment. However, careful ventilation is essential to prevent the fumes given off by the heater harming the emerging seedlings.

WATERING

Watering with a fine-rosed watering can is by far the most reliable way of irrigating your plants provided you can spare the time and have the energy to carry water around all day long. There won't be time either for holidays or even weekends away from the hustle and bustle of watering a greenhouse by hand. Of course, all this time spent in the greenhouse holding a watering can isn't entirely wasted because you can take the opportunity of

---

SETTING UP A CAPILLARY WATERING SYSTEM STEP-BY-STEP

1. Make sure your bench is sturdy, flat and level. Then lay a sheet of heavy-duty black polythene on the bench.

2. Lay a sheet of capillary matting on top of the black polythene and cut to size. Stand temporary pots and seedtrays directly on top of this.

3. For permanent pot plants, cover the capillary matting with black polythene to prevent evaporation and the build-up of algae. Cut a hole for each pot.

4. If you want to make it semi-automatic, allow one end of the capillary matting to dangle over one end into a trough which can be filled with water. The trough can then be topped up as needed.

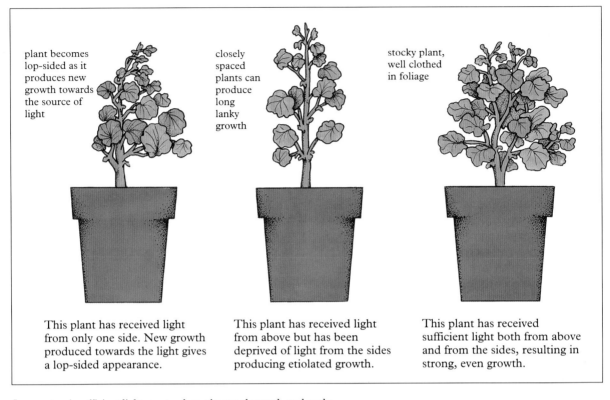

plant becomes
lop-sided as it
produces new
growth towards
the source of
light

closely
spaced
plants can
produce
long
lanky
growth

stocky plant,
well clothed
in foliage

This plant has received light
from only one side. New growth
produced towards the light gives
a lop-sided appearance.

This plant has received light
from above but has been
deprived of light from the sides
producing etiolated growth.

This plant has received
sufficient light both from above
and from the sides, resulting in
strong, even growth.

*Incorrect or insufficient light can produce abnormal growth and make
plants more susceptible to pest and disease problems.*

studying each and every plant at close quarters.
Check for pests, diseases, sideshoots, flowerbuds
and developing fruits; this enables quick action
when problems occur.

There are many watering systems available to
reduce plants' dependence on gardeners. Some are
partially automatic – with reservoirs which need
topping up regularly – and there is now a trend
towards completely independent, computer-
operated systems that can be left alone once set up
except for a few checks each week.

They can be fitted with seep hoses that are
suitable for watering rows, trickle or drip systems
that can be used for watering individual plants
in pots or in the ground, or a capillary watering
system for pots only.

The main advantages of an automatic system are
that they save a lot of time, let plants have the water
when they need it, and can be set up to allow you
to go away on holiday without worrying.

LIGHTING

It is no secret that plants need light to grow and prosper. In summer this isn't a problem with natural
light levels far exceeding the plants' requirements
even on dull, overcast days. In winter, however, light
levels can be too low for healthy growth and weakened
plants become susceptible to pests and diseases.

Supplementary lighting is the remedy. String up
a series of growing lamps to supplement low light
levels and extend the day length. The latter is particularly important with some plants, like chrysanthemums, that need specific periods of light and
dark before they will produce flowerbuds.

Unfortunately, any old lightbulb will not satisfy
the plant's needs – ordinary household bulbs emit
only part of the light spectrum that plants require,
so special growing bulbs are needed. Several manufacturers supply specially designed bulbs for
plants, indoors and outside in the greenhouse.

CHAPTER 4

Compost and Containers

COMPOSTS

To a novice, choosing a compost can be one of the most confusing aspects of greenhouse gardening. It is the life-support medium for all container-grown plants, so it's worth spending a little time to understand the fundamentals.

Many years ago professional gardeners would take great pride in their composts, altering the composition to suit every plant in the garden perfectly. Unfortunately, this took a lifetime's experience to get right and these composts became some of the gardener's most closely guarded secrets. It was a very wasteful method of growing with trial and error experiments being performed up and down the country by countless individuals trying to achieve the same result.

The John Innes Horticultural Institute, therefore, decided to set up a series of scientifically controlled experiments to develop a range of standard composts that would pander to the needs of all container-grown plants. After a long series of experiments they came up with a range of composts: John Innes seed compost (J.I.S.) for sowing, and three potting composts containing varying amounts of fertilizer to suit the demands of different plants. John Innes No. 1 is for potting up seedlings into their first 3½in (9cm) pot. (It can also be used for sowing strong growing plants such as sweet peas.) John Innes No. 2 is for potting the majority of plants and John Innes No. 3 for demanding plants such as tomatoes. Formulated over fifty years ago, these mixtures are still going strong.

Over thirty years ago, the potential for peat-based composts was identified by commercial growers who wanted a rooting medium that they could rely on. Peat provides the right rooting conditions with a balance between water holding capability and air content. Sand was added to give the compost some weight. Peat and sand contain no plant nutrients, so these had to be added in the form of fertilizer. With such simple ingredients it was possible to manufacture a consistent compost ideal for the plants being grown.

In recent years, conservationists have highlighted the potential damage of widespread peat extraction from wetlands. This has lead to a spate of new composts being developed based either on low-peat formulations or on non-peat alternatives such as coir, composted bark and other waste products from the timber industry.

You can make your own composts (*see* DIY Compost Recipes, overleaf) but you will have to make quite a lot and it will probably work out more expensive than buying ready-made. For a quick and cheap homemade loam-based compost, mix a bucketful of good garden soil with a bucketful of well-rotted manure and add a handful of balanced fish, blood and bone fertilizer. If you want a

Gloxinia.

Kalonchoë.

---

well-drained compost add up to bucketful of sharp sand (depending on how clayey your soil is). Mix thoroughly and use. Do not store composts from season to season as they deteriorate quickly.

MAKING YOUR OWN COMPOST

Loam-based Compost Ingredients

Loam
A good friable garden soil from a well-cultivated vegetable plot would do, or for best results stack turves upside down to rot. All loam should be sieved and sterilized before use otherwise you will be overrun with weeds.

Peat
Use a bale of ordinary horticultural grade moss or sedge peat – not too fine or too coarse. It should be slightly moist. Well-rotted leafmould is an acceptable substitute.

Sand
Use a gritty sharp sand that has angular corners – made from graded crushed rock. Don't be tempted to use yellow builders' sand or any other that has

Aphelandra.

DIY LOAM-BASED COMPOST RECIPES

If you feel you would like to mix your own compost, here are the basic recipes.

Remember, a bushel is a dry measure of 8 gallons (36 litres) or four 2 gallon (9 litre) bucketfuls.

BASIC INGREDIENTS OF POTTING COMPOST

7 parts sterilized loam
3 parts peat
2 parts sharp sand

JOHN INNES POTTING COMPOST NO. 1

To each bushel of basic ingredients add:
¾oz (21g) ground limestone or chalk
4oz (113g) John Innes base fertilizer

JOHN INNES POTTING COMPOST NO. 2

To each bushel of basic ingredients add:
1½oz (42g) ground limestone or chalk
8oz (227g) John Innes base fertilizer

JOHN INNES POTTING COMPOST NO. 3

To each bushel of basic ingredients add:
2¼oz (63g) ground limestone or chalk
12oz (336g) John Innes base fertilizer

JOHN INNES SEED COMPOST

2 parts sterilized loam
1 part peat
1 part sharp sand

To each bushel add:
1½oz (42g) superphosphate
¾oz (21g) ground limestone or chalk
John Innes base fertilizer is available ready-made from most horticultural retailers or it can be made from the following recipe:

2 parts hoof and horn
2 parts superphosphate
1 part sulphate of potash

Fertilizers
These are widely available from garden centres and horticultural supply shops.

John Innes recipes are based on good garden loam which in time has become increasingly difficult to obtain and, of course, more expensive. This has resulted in further research that has led to the development of a new range of composts based not on loam but on peat.

Peat-based Compost Ingredients

Peat
This medium provides the necessary water retention and aeration in the compost. It is a variable commodity available from many locations up and down the country, and so is usually blended to give a consistent product. Choose a graded moss or sedge peat available in bales.

Sand
Sand gives the compost weight and is now thought to help the re-wetting of compost once it has dried out. Use only angular horticultural grade sand.

Lime
Lime is essential to counter the inherent acidity of many peats. Too much acidity will cause nutrients to be 'locked-up' and unavailable to plants.

Fertilizers
Any medium devoid of natural nutrients must have nitrogen, phosphorus and potash. However, it is also important to add trace elements like iron, manganese, zinc, boron and molybdenum which are needed by plants in minute quantities.

Environmentally Friendly Composts

Since 1988 manufacturers have been working on composts that require no peat. It takes a long time to perfect a new compost, so manufacturers have introduced a range of low-peat composts as a stopgap measure to satisfy consumer demand. As the name suggests, a low-peat compost contains a lot less peat than a conventional peat-based one: another medium such as composted bark is

been produced naturally by the forces of erosion. These sands have more rounded corners and so they compact together reducing aeration as well as the ability to drain.

PEAT-BASED COMPOSTS

By far the most common type of compost sold today is peat based. They can be split into three basic types: sowing, potting and general purpose. These vary mainly in their level of nutrients with sowing compost having the least, potting compost having the most and general purpose being a compromise between the two.

PROS

❀ Good for seedlings and young plants.
❀ Good aeration.
❀ Good water retention.
❀ Free from pests and diseases.
❀ Light to handle.
❀ Clean.

CONS

❀ Leaching can be a problem.
❀ Top-heavy subjects tend to topple.
❀ Need careful watering and feeding.

DIY PEAT-BASED COMPOST RECIPES

SEED COMPOST

1 part peat
1 part sharp sand

To each bushel of ingredients add:
   ½oz (14g) sulphate of ammonia
   1oz (28g) superphosphate
   ½oz (14g) sulphate of potash
   4oz (113g) ground limestone or chalk

POTTING COMPOST

3 parts peat
1 part sharp sand

To each bushel of ingredients add:
   ½oz (14g) sulphate of ammonia
   ½oz (14g) urea-formaldehyde (38 per cent nitrogen)
   2oz (56g) superphosphate
   1oz (28g) sulphate of potash
   4oz (113g) ground limestone or chalk
   2oz (56g) dolomite limestone
   plus fritted trace elements

Gerbera.

substituted for up to two-thirds of the peat.

There are a number of waste-products being evaluated by manufacturers for their potential as a base for compost, but the two that have shown most promise are coir and bark.

Coir is a waste-product of the coconut industry which has accumulated over many years in great heaps in countries such as Sri Lanka, in and around the Indian Ocean. Although early indications are that it can make a good substitute for peat, it is more expensive and supplies are limited. It also doesn't make much sense on environmental grounds because it has to be moved half-way around the world, using up fuel, and in any case, should be incorporated back into local soils to maintain their fertility.

Bark is a waste product of the timber industry and a number of useful products have been developed such as soil conditioners and mulches. Once stripped from the trees bark has to be composted to drive off volatile oils and kill off fungi spores and insects. Again early indications show that composted bark can make an effective compost especially when mixed with some peat. However, it is more expensive than peat and it is unlikely there will be sufficient to meet demand.

Cacti require a compost that will hold moisture during the growing season.

Other potential waste-products that could be turned into compost include animal wastes, sewage and straw. Straw and animal manure has long been the basic ingredients for farmyard manure and is an excellent soil improver once thoroughly composted. But as yet there are too many problems with contamination from heavy metals and diseases to make sewage into a reliable and safe compost.

Specialist Composts

A range of specialist composts have been developed for those plants that don't grow well in the basic mediums. Ericaceous, alpine, orchid and cactus are the main ones.

Ericaceous is the most important of these and caters for those plants, like rhododendrons, azaleas and many heathers, that prefer an acidic growing medium.

Alpines are very sensitive to wet conditions and so need a well-drained compost to prevent waterlogging. Orchid compost also needs to be very free draining with plenty of air spaces, while cacti needs a compost that can hold moisture when the plants are actively growing and yet be allowed to dry out when they are not.

CONTAINERS

Like composts, containers have been revolutionized in recent years. Traditionally, clay pots and wooden seedtrays were used, but with the advent of cheaper, cleaner plastic these stalwart materials have all but disappeared.

Pots

It is a shame that clay pots are an expensive rarity nowadays, since they offer a significant advantage over their plastic rival. It really all comes down to the clay's porous nature – allowing much needed air in to the compost and encouraging a more humid atmosphere around the pot by allowing water to escape in the form of vapour. This produces a happier and healthier growing environment. Cheap plastic pots have now taken over. They are easy to handle and clean, which is a great advantage during the busy spring period. In addition, plastic pots take up very little storage space. The following are a few of the advantages each material has to offer.

Plastic

- ❀ Cheap.
- ❀ Easy to clean.
- ❀ Wide range of styles available.
- ❀ Light and easy to store.
- ❀ Some designs almost unbreakable.

Geranium seedlings grow well in modular seedtrays.

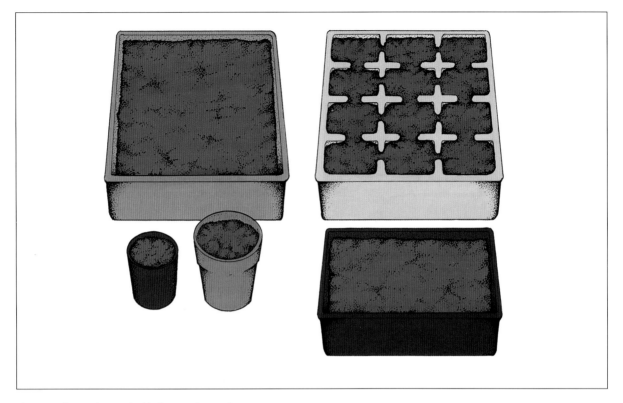

A range of containers suitable for growing seed.

Clay

- ❀ Porous.
- ❀ Looks good and blends in.
- ❀ Provides stability.
- ❀ Good growing environment.

Seedtrays

Old-fashioned wooden seedtrays were heavy, took a lot of valuable storage space and were almost impossible to sterilize effectively. The plastic alternative doesn't suffer from any of these drawbacks, although they rarely survive more than a couple of seasons in my garden.

Furthermore, recent designs compartmentalizing the seedtray into modules are a real boon when you are trying to get your seedlings off to the best possible start by not disturbing the roots when potting on. The only previous alternative was to put each one in its own pot – and who has the space for that?

GROWING BAGS

Growing bags are an ideal way of raising cucumbers and tomatoes in the greenhouse. They are widely available, very cheap and on the whole reliable. Make sure a bargain bag contains the same amount of compost as a standard growing bag if you want to grow two or three tomato plants. Also, avoid any bags that have become waterlogged or look faded as they may be old stock from last year.

When transported and stored in the retail outlet, growing bags are stacked which inevitably leads to the compost being compacted. So, before planting plump up the bag like a pillow to loosen the compost.

Make the most of your growing bag by raising hungry and demanding plants such as tomatoes in the first year, then the following season or overwinter grow a less demanding crop such as lettuce, and finally spread the used compost as a mulch over the soil or incorporate as a soil conditioner.

CHAPTER 5

Propagation

Few things are more satisfying to a gardener than the propagation of plants. To see something grow from a simple seed or cutting and develop, with tender loving care, to fruitful maturity, gives a real sense of achievement. Although all this can be done without a greenhouse, indeed without a garden at all, the range of plants you can propagate will be severely curtailed if you don't have the right growing environment. Furthermore, once you have caught the propagation fever you'll want to try your hand at everything.

HOW TO SOW MOST SEED STEP-BY-STEP

1. Select a container that has plenty of drainage holes and one that is not too deep – the more compost you use the more expensive the operation.

2. Fill your seedtray with seed compost (either loam-based or peat-based) and spread it out evenly with your finger tips to ensure there are no air holes.

3. Firm the compost lightly with a flat presser – either home-made from wood or a shop-bought version. If you're sowing in pots use the base of another pot to firm with.

4. Water the compost thoroughly using a fine-rosed watering can. Make sure the rose is pointing upwards so the water cascades gently onto the compost without disturbing the surface. Check that the rose doesn't dribble and rut the compost.

5. Leave the watered seedtrays for fifteen minutes or so, to drain excess water.

6. Sow the seed thinly and evenly over the surface of the compost. To achieve this fold one edge of the seed packet to form a V-shape, then hold the packet level in one hand and tap it gently with the forefinger of the other. Alternatively, pour the contents of the seed packet into one palm, cupping it a few inches above the prepared seedtray. Then tap it gently with the other hand. Both these methods should allow a continuous stream of seeds dropping singly onto the compost.

MATERIALS FOR PROPAGATION

POTS

Plastic 3½in pots are the most versatile because you can use them for sowing or rooting cuttings direct and then use the same size pot for potting up seedlings and young plants. Smaller pots contain less compost and so are prone to drying out quickly and larger ones hold too much compost that becomes wet and stagnant as well as the pots taking a lot more valuable compost and bench space. Other pots worth buying include: 6in pots for potting on plants that have become established in their 3½in pots; half-depth pots or pans for sowing tiny seed; and peat pots for plants, such as French beans, that hate root disturbance. For tap-rooted seedlings such as sweetpeas use bottomless long pots.

SEEDTRAYS

Standard 14 × 8½in seedtrays are the most useful for sowing bedding plants that will be needed in fairly large numbers. Half-trays are worth having for sowing smaller amounts of seed. Compartmentalized seedtrays are useful for larger seed (sow two per compartment and thin out the weakest) or plants that resent root disturbance.

SHARP KNIFE OR SECATEURS

A straight-edged propagation knife is only necessary if you take a lot of cuttings as it is easy to keep clean and sharp. If you just want to take a few cuttings use a sharp pair of secateurs. If your secatures are not in good enough condition use a craft knife instead.

CLEAR POLYTHENE BAGS

Essential for collecting cutting material as it prevents material wilting and different plants can be separated and labelled in different bags. Clear freezer bags are ideal as they have a panel for labelling.

FRESH COMPOST

Choose a good quality compost and use it fresh. Old compost will inevitably result in failure. For sowing it is essential that the compost is fine-textured without lumps (see Chapter 4).

SIEVE

The only sure way of covering seed with a light and even layer of compost is to use a sieve to disperse it.

WATERING CAN

To keep the compost moist after sowing it is essential to have a watering can with a fine rose. Fit the rose upside-down so that you get a gentle shower of water that does not disturb the compost surface or flatten any of the seedlings.

GLASS OR CLINGFILM

Traditional method of keeping seed moist after sowing is to cover the seedtray with a pane of glass and a sheet of newspaper to keep out the light. The newspaper needs to be removed as the first seedlings germinate and the glass a day or two later. The modern alternative to glass is clingfilm. A pane of glass also makes an easy to clean and hard surface on which to prepare cuttings.

DIBBER

Simply a blunt tool for making the holes for sowing large seed individually, as well as separating and transplanting seedlings. A pencil is ideal.

LABELS AND A PENCIL

Recording information about what you have sown and when is essential if you are to keep on top of sowing in the spring. Always label when you sow or take cuttings. It's also worth noting on the seed packet the date of the previous sowing for those crops that are sown at regular intervals throughout the spring and early summer.

ROOTING HORMONE

This is useful for promoting root development on any plants that are difficult to root from cuttings. Easy-to-root plants such as geraniums don't need rooting hormone.

DISINFECTANT

After potting on plants from pots and trays, the containers should be cleaned with a garden disinfectant to sterilize them. Also sterilize the blades of knives and secateurs before use.

SOWING SEED THAT NEEDS LIGHT STEP-BY-STEP

1. After following Steps 1 and 2 of 'Sowing Medium-sized Seed' (*see* next page), sprinkle seeds thinly on the surface of the compost by tapping hand gently.

2. Cover seed with a thin layer of translucent vermiculite.

3. Label clearly with a waterproof pen, stating variety sown and the date of sowing.

4. Place the seedtray in a propagator set at the correct temperature for the seed sown.

SOWING FINE SEED STEP-BY-STEP

1. Mix the fine seed with dry silver sand. This will enable you to sow the seed evenly.

2. Sprinkle mix on the surface of moist compost. Do not cover.

3. Label clearly with waterproof pen.

4. Cover with a pane of glass, on top of which should be placed a sheet of newspaper.

SEED

Although sowing seed is a very simple operation, there are several variations to the technique depending on the size of the seed and whether or not it requires light to germinate.

For very fine seed, such as begonia, lobelia, petunia, calceolaria and gloxinia, introduce some fine, dry silver sand into the seed packet. Mixed thoroughly with the seed, it acts as a spreading agent when the seed is sown in the normal way.

Large seeds can be sown individually into pots of seed compost. Make a hole with a pencil or small dibber, place one seed in each hole and then top up the hole with compost.

SOWING MEDIUM-SIZED SEED STEP-BY-STEP

1. Fill the seedtray with fresh sowing compost and level.
2. Lightly firm with a block, or the base of another seedtray.
3. Space five rows of eight seeds on the surface of the compost.
4. Cover seeds with a thin, even layer of sieved compost.
5. Label clearly with a waterproof pen, stating variety sown and the date of sowing.

SOWING LARGE SEED STEP-BY-STEP

1. Fill seed modules with seed compost. Place a seed on top of the compost and gently push it beneath the surface sowing one seed per module. Label clearly with a waterproof pen (far left), recording the name of the variety sown and the date of sowing.

2. Water after sowing large seed to help settle the compost around the seed and eliminate air-pockets.

SOWING AFTERCARE STEP-BY-STEP

1. Label the seedtray carefully.

2. Cover the tray with a clean sheet of glass and a sheet of newspaper. This will keep warmth and humidity in and light, mice and next door's cat out.

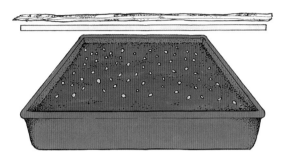

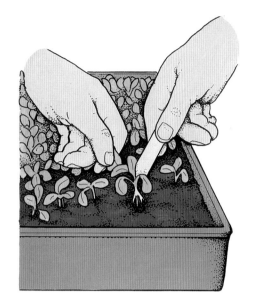

3. Place in a warm position, out of direct sunlight – usually 64–70°F (18–21°C). Check the directions on the seed packet or in the seed company's catalogue.

4. Check the seedtrays every day if possible – remove the newspaper and glass as soon as seedlings emerge. Then move the seedtray to a light position out of direct sunlight so that the seedlings don't become drawn and spindly.

   The first leaves to appear are the so called seed leaves. These nurture the seedling through its first few days until it produces its first true leaves.

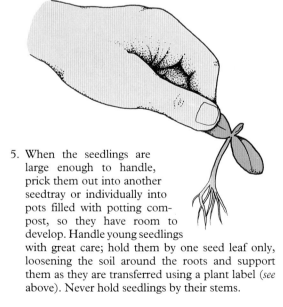

5. When the seedlings are large enough to handle, prick them out into another seedtray or individually into pots filled with potting compost, so they have room to develop. Handle young seedlings with great care; hold them by one seed leaf only, loosening the soil around the roots and support them as they are transferred using a plant label (*see* above). Never hold seedlings by their stems.

6. Water in thoroughly and replace into a light position out of direct sunlight.

Cover surface-sown seeds with a layer of seed compost to prevent them drying out. To get an even coverage use a sieve. The depth of compost cover required will depend entirely on the type of seed you're sowing, so check the seed packet for directions. However, if you have collected your own seed or if the packet has been mislaid then a rough guide is to cover the seed with a depth of compost equal to the width of the seed. Dust-fine seed should not be covered at all.

VEGETATIVE PROPAGATION

When viable seed is not available for one reason or another, or when plants don't grow true to type from the seed they produce, then they have to be propagated by vegetative means. Basically this method consists of taking a part of one individual and encouraging that part to produce a self-supporting root system and become an individual in its own right. Several methods are used in the greenhouse, including stem cuttings, leaf cuttings, layering and division.

Softwood Cuttings

Softwood cuttings are so-called because they are taken from current year's growth in spring and summer that has not had time to ripen and produce a woody outer layer. A wide range of plants, including dahlias, chrysanthemums and fuchsias can be increased in this way (*see* picture sequence right).
* Select healthy, strong, non-flowering shoots of current year's growth. Cut the shoots cleanly from the plant just above a leaf joint (node) using a sharp knife.
* At the work bench, trim up the cuttings, making your cut just below a node so that the final cutting is around 3in (7.5cm) long.
* Trim off the lower leaves close to the stem and remove any immature flowerbuds.
* Dip the cut end of each cutting into a little hormone rooting powder or liquid and tap it lightly to remove excess.
* Fill a container with compost and firm, lightly covering the surface with a little silver sand to aid drainage around each cutting.
* Make a hole in the prepared compost using a

small dibber and insert the cuttings to about half their length.
* Firm and water.
* Cover with clear polythene bag and seal with tie or elastic bag.

Semi-ripe Cuttings

When shoots have developed a woody layer at their base in mid- to late summer, they are said to be semi-ripe. Many garden trees and shrubs can be propagated using this method (*see* picture sequence overleaf).
* Select healthy side shoots of the current year's growth 4 to 5in (10 and 12.5cm) long. Tear the

Softwood Cuttings

1. Trim each cutting just below a node (above).

2. Remove lower leaves close to the stem (above centre).

3. Insert prepared cuttings (above far right).

4. Firm in cuttings and water; clearly label (right).

5. Cover pot of cuttings with clear polythene bag (far right).

Semi-ripe Cuttings

1. Pull cuttings off with a woody heel and trim using a sharp knife or razor blade if necessary (above left).
2. Dip cut ends in hormone rooting powder (above right).

3. Insert cuttings around the edge of a container; firm, clearly label and water (below left).
4. Cover with a clear polythene bag (below right).

side shoot from the branch by bending it back-wards towards the main stem of the parent plant. This will produce a short snag of woody material (known as a heel) from the parent that needs to be trimmed up using a sharp knife. Longer sideshoots should be cut from the parent plant cleanly, then trimmed back to about 4in (10cm).

❀ Remove the lower leaves and reduce the leaf area of large-leaved plants by cutting each leaf back by half.

❀ Dip the bottom of each cutting in hormone rooting powder, specially prepared for semi-ripe cuttings and shake off excess.

❀ Insert prepared cuttings around the edge of a container filled with compost and dusted with silver sand.

❀ Firm, label, and water.

❀ Cover with clear polythene bag and seal with tie or elastic band.

Leaf cuttings

There are several types of leaf cutting. Which method you use will depend on the plant being propagated. Saintpaulias, for instance are increased by taking leaf and stalk cuttings.

How to take Saintpaulia Leaf Cuttings

1. Select a healthy, strong leaf that has developed fully but is not too old. Cut it cleanly from its parent using a sharp knife, making sure no stump is left that could rot back.

HOW TO TAKE *BEGONIA REX* WHOLE LEAF CUTTINGS STEP-BY-STEP

1. Select a young, healthy leaf that is fully developed and remove it cleanly at the point it joins the parent plant.

2. Remove the stalk, then lay it on a flat surface before making several short cuts across the main veins – each about ½in (1.25cm) long and about an inch or so apart. Dust each with hormone rooting powder.

3. Lay the leaf flat on the surface of moist cuttings compost, pressing it gently with your palm to get the cuts in good contact with the compost. Scatter a few small stones or something equally weighty to keep the leaf flat, or peg it down with bent pins.

4. Careful watering is important to prevent the rather exposed leaf from shrivelling.

5. Plantlets will form in a few weeks if all is well and these should be potted on singly into 3½in (9cm) pots using a potting compost.

2. Trim up the leaf stalk to about 1in (2.5cm) long, then insert into a pot of moist compost so that the stalk is about half buried.
3. Firm well.
4. Water saintpaulia cuttings carefully making sure that no water gets onto the hairy leaves because they have a tendency to rot.
5. Soon roots will form and new plantlets will appear at the base of the old leaf stalks. When these plantlets are large enough to handle, they should be potted up singly. The old leaf stalk should be discarded.

How to take Streptocarpus Leaf Blade Cuttings
1. Choose a healthy, fully developed leaf and trim it from the parent.
2. Cut the leaf into sections: either in two longitudinally (removing the midrib), or laterally into several 1in (2.5cm) sections.
3. Dust hormone rooting powder over the cut ends to be inserted into the compost.
4. Place longitudinal cuttings into shallow slits made in the surface of the compost so that they stick up like shark fins.
5. Insert lateral sections leaving two-thirds of each standing proud of the compost.

6. Plantlets develop around the cut ends of veins, but can take some time to appear. Keep compost moist and mist cuttings to prevent them drying out. When large enough, carefully separate the new plantlets and pot up individually.

Air Layering

Air layering is not a way of multiplying your stock quickly like the other methods already discussed. It is a technique you can turn to when your aralia or rubber plant gets too big or when it has dropped all its leaves and the bare stem is beginning to look unsightly.

❀ Using a sharp, sturdy knife make a 2in (5cm) upward incision a few inches below the last leaf so that the cut runs at an angle halfway through the stem. Support the stem with a cane.
❀ Place a matchstick in the cut to hold it open while it is dusted with hormone rooting powder.
❀ Remove the matchstick and replace with a handful of sphagnum moss.
❀ Pack moss around the cut, forming a ball of moss around the stem. Then cover in polythene.
❀ Seal the polythene at both ends, using adhesive tape.

Air Layering
1. Make a 2in (5cm) upward incision (left).
2. After dusting with hormone-rooting powder, place sphagnum moss in the cut (centre).
3. Cover the cut and moss in polythene and seal with tape.

Orchids can be propagated by division.

❀ When a good growth of roots can be seen in the ball of moss, the main stem of the parent plant can be cut through just below the roots and the resulting rooted top half of the plant potted up.

Division

Many multi-stemmed or clump-forming plants like ferns, orchids, agapanthus and aspidistra can be multiplied using this method. When in need of repotting in spring a pot-bound plant can be split into two or more sections, depending on its size – each with at least one plump bud and its own portion of the root system.

1. Water the plant to be divided, then leave it to drain for twenty-four hours.
2. Remove pot and any drainage crocks, then tease the roots apart, removing the compost as you go.
3. If the clump cannot be pulled apart by hand or where there's a crown, use a sharp knife to separate sections.
4. Dust larger cut surfaces with a powdered fungicide such as 'flowers of sulphur'. Then repot individually making sure

the growing point remains just showing at the surface after firming. With very old plants the original central section may have to be discarded.

Saintpaulias can be propagated by division or by leaf cuttings.

CHAPTER 6

Spring

GENERAL MANAGEMENT

Early Spring

The first month of spring, it is said, comes in like a lion and goes out like a lamb. True or not, it is often a stormy month with the odd week or so of fine weather. In the greenhouse the permanent staging provides the backbone of colour during this month with the beautiful and varied species of *Primula*, such as *malacoides, kewensis, obconia* and *sinensis*. Lovely colour combinations and delicate fragrance of recent introductions has lead to a revival of this underrated pot plant.

Space will soon become a limiting factor in the greenhouse. It is, therefore, worth spending a little

The Pyrenean primrose should be propagated by division in spring, or by leaf cuttings taken in summer.

time at the beginning of spring to erect extra temporary staging and shelving to double, treble or even quadruple the available growing space. Use the permanent staging, if any, for pot plants, and a propagator. Keep any recently sown seedtrays underneath, but don't stack them up otherwise you will find it difficult to check for germination. As seeds germinate, move them out into a light position, using the temporary staging and shelving.

The lengthening days and warmer, sunny spells will make maintaining a constant temperature in the greenhouse a challenge. A couple of hours of midday sun can send the temperatures soaring, yet an overcast day can be cold and dingy. Ventilation is the only means of controlling rises in temperature at this time of year, so an automatic vent is essential unless you intend spending all day, every day in the greenhouse.

Use a maximum/minimum thermometer to check the automatic vent is set correctly and also make sure the constant opening and closing hasn't upset the tight fitting of the vents when shut. Cold draughts can be very damaging to soft, young shoots.

Continue to check heaters on a regular basis right through this month. For the majority of greenhouse crops aim for a temperature of around 45°F (7°C) at night and 61°F (16°C) during the day. This rise should not be allowed to occur in one go but in several stages throughout the morning by careful ventilation, followed by a similarly gradual decrease during the afternoon.

Watering will be more frequent but in early spring far less critical. Water regularly, keeping a careful check on those seedlings with small root systems and plants in small volumes of compost – those in modular seedtrays, for instance. Time taken watering will be ever-increasing through the

EARLY SPRING QUICK REFERENCE CHECKLIST

Sow sweetpeas in early to mid-spring for a summer display of colour.

❀ Ventilate as required.
❀ Check temperatures regularly.
❀ Maintain heating equipment.

FLOWERS

❀ Sow many annuals, biennials, perennials, cacti, fuchsias and geraniums.
❀ Prick out seedlings as necessary.
❀ Continue to take chrysanthemum, dahlia and fuchsia cuttings.
❀ Divide border dahlia tubers.
❀ Pot on early carnations and chrysanthemum cuttings.
❀ Harden off autumn-struck cuttings.
❀ Plant tuberous begonias and cannas.

VEGETABLES

❀ Make successional sowings of salad vegetables.
❀ Sow herbs, summer cabbage, cauliflowers and winter celery.
❀ Sow melons, cucumbers, sweet peppers and aubergines as well as tomatoes for unheated greenhouses and outside.

DISEASES

Keep an eye open for damping off disease, which causes seedlings to topple over like felled trees. Where it occurs, remove affected seedlings and water others with a solution of Cheshunt Compound. Hygiene is most important in early spring. If pests and diseases become established they'll plague your efforts all summer long. Take the necessary remedial action to combat invaders as soon as possible – delay will often mean repeat sprays and loss of crop vigour.

Fumigation is often worth while early on. Not only does it clear the greenhouse of unwanted visitors, but the smoke will pinpoint any leaks in the greenhouse structures.

spring and summer, so perhaps it would be worth considering some form of automatic assistance. Capillary matting on the bench is an effective way of watering established pot plants and the drip or dribble automatic irrigation systems are ideal for watering growing bags or plants grown in the border soil (*see also* Chapter 3).

Mid-spring

This time in the season is full of surprises as far as the weather is concerned. It often brings hail, snow, sunshine and showers all in one month. Warm days and freezing nights make greenhouse gardening difficult. The middle of the month usually brings sunshine and showers, but thunderstorms, too, can prevail so cautious ventilation is essential.

There are often conflicting interests, with some plants requiring constant heat and others needing to be hardened off. In a large greenhouse this can be achieved by sectioning off areas with insulative bubble plastic, but in smaller ones it is much more difficult. A simple answer is to invest in a frame that can be given bottom heat in the form of soil-warming cables. Use this to harden off plants destined for the garden by gradually reducing the growing temperature and increasing ventilation. This will leave the greenhouse free for heat-demanding crops.

Alternatively you can take advantage of the temperature variations that occur within even a small greenhouse. For instance, those plants that need

MID-SPRING QUICK REFERENCE CHECKLIST

❀ Check heaters and ventilators.
❀ Apply shading where necessary.
❀ Check for pests and diseases.

FLOWERS

❀ Sow annuals, biennials and perennials.
❀ Sow primroses, polyanthus and pot-grown primulas.
❀ Divide border dahlias.

❀ Plant achimenes and amaryllis.
❀ Stop chrysanthemums.
❀ Repot house and greenhouse plants.
❀ Plant baskets.

VEGETABLES

❀ Sow melons, cucumbers and tomatoes for outdoor cultivation.
❀ Sow sweetcorn, marrows, courgettes, runner-beans and French beans.
❀ Space early tomatoes.
❀ Plant cucumbers and melons in an unheated greenhouse.

FRUIT

❀ Start vines in an unheated greenhouse.
❀ Pollinate early starters.
❀ Thin peaches and nectarines.
❀ Pollinate strawberries.

Propagate saintpaulias in mid-spring.

hardening off can be left under the influence of the cool air spilling through the vents saving the warmer greenhouse staging for seedlings and other tender subjects. This system, though, takes a lot more looking after and checking.

Heating is becoming less critical at night as the frequency of freezing temperatures lessens. However, it's easy to become complacent. Whatever the weatherman says, check the greenhouse every day to make sure all is well.

Ventilation becomes easier to sustain and, in fact, is essential to keep temperatures down during mild, sunny spells in mid-spring. Just keep using the ridge vents, though, and don't be tempted to open anything lower down since it could spell disaster. Aim for a maximum daytime temperature of about 70°F (21°C).

Shading is sometimes necessary in mid-spring, but only the temporary kind. Bubble matting is particularly useful at this time of year because it gives partial shading during the day and prevents cooling at night. Just pin it up on the south-facing side to keep out the strongest rays.

Watering will be more critical as many plants get into top gear as far as growing is concerned. Those still in small pots or yet to be pricked out of seed-trays are particularly vulnerable, so they must be checked each day.

With the new growth on many plants comes the threat of pest and disease attack. Check all crops as they are being watered for signs of damage or indications of other problems. Pests like aphids and spider mite can build up in numbers very quickly if left unchecked.

Late Spring

Much of the work associated with the greenhouse at this time of the season is outside in the garden, preparing areas for planting out greenhouse raised plants; clearing beds, borders and the vegetable plot as well as refurbishing tubs, troughs, hanging baskets and windowboxes.

Slugs can be a real problem about this time with young, soft plants being exposed to the big wide world. Before trying to combat them, however, scan the garden to see if there are any piles of rotting debris lying around. These moist, cool hideaways are ideal for slugs, so any dead or dying organic matter should be dispatched to the compost heap with haste.

Crossandra

Late spring often sees the first really hot days of the year and so precautions must be taken to protect susceptible plants in the greenhouse. This is complicated somewhat since the first couple of weeks can also see frosty nights that catch out the unwary gardener. Protect plants on sunny days with temporary shading material. It is still too early to erect any permanent cover since overcast days can be dreary indeed. Netting materials on the outside of the greenhouse, or adjustable blinds on the inside, are ideal and can be used on cold nights to insulate the greenhouse.

Heating is needed less now, but on the nights it is required it is crucial. It is important, therefore, to check the heater regularly throughout late spring.

LATE SPRING QUICK REFERENCE CHECKLIST

❀ Prepare beds for planting out bedding.
❀ Check for pests and disease.
❀ Water and shade where necessary.

FLOWERS

❀ Harden off bedding and other plants destined for the garden.
❀ Plant out bedding.
❀ Sow cinerarias.
❀ Prick out seedlings as they become large enough.
❀ Pot on rooted cuttings.
❀ Plant out chrysanthemums.
❀ Put freesias, nerines, lachenalias and arum lilies to rest for the summer.
❀ Train fuchsias.

VEGETABLES

❀ Harden off sweet peppers and aubergines.
❀ Plant tomatoes in unheated greenhouses.
❀ Train early cucumbers.

FRUIT

❀ Train and pollinate vines and thin early starters.

Gardeners who rely on paraffin will be having sleepless nights on those occasions that the heater is considered unnecessary. Paraffin heaters will also be wasteful on nights when a couple of hours heat is needed because they will be burning all night long.

Ventilation will not be so much of a problem this month. It will be possible to ventilate most days and even a little on mild nights. Use the roof vents only at night – not utilizing side vents except on very warm, relatively calm days. Cold draughts can still cause problems.

BEWARE

The risk of late frosts still persists right through spring, so cautious hardening off and planting out are essential. The weather is generally less predictable, so keep an eye on forecasts since a late cold snap can ruin all your efforts in the garden.

Watering will remain vitally important throughout late spring with the increased periods of sunshine and high temperatures coupled with vigorous growth. Many plants will need watering every day but by no means all. Therefore, a check on each plant will be necessary each day – a rota will soon surface. Vigorous plants like tomatoes, melons and cucumbers will need a lot of water as will early vines, peaches and nectarines, to swell their developing fruit. Also check pot plants and seedtrays, since their limited volume of growing medium will dry out very quickly. Here watering several times a day will be needed, unless an automatic watering system has been installed.

There are a number of automatic or semi-automatic watering systems on the market that are worth considering if you do not have the time available to concentrate on the demanding spring and summer greenhouse (*see* Chapter 3).

Constantly scan all crops for outbreaks of pests and diseases. In particular, check the undersides of tomato and cucumber leaves for whitefly and spider mite (*see also* Pests and Diseases).

Clear debris from the greenhouse after the frantic sowing and potting season. Collect together used labels, pots and seedtrays ready for cleaning and storing.

Most plants in the greenhouse, indeed throughout the garden, will be in rapid growth and so require regular feeding.

PROPAGATION

Flowers

The pace of sowing is at its peak in early spring, so it is prudent to have a system worked out in advance to utilize diminishing shelf and staging areas to best effect. A rotation system can be effective so that seedlings of different ages don't get mixed up and left to grow too big before pricking out or potting on.

Sowing begins in earnest in early spring, so get yourself organized. Early sowings of sweet peas are followed by geraniums and herbs as well as half-hardy annuals, greenhouse annuals, herbaceous perennials and many alpines.

White regal pelargonium.

Check seedlings regularly for germination – at least once a day. At the first signs that seedlings are starting to emerge, remove the seedtray from the relative darkness of lower staging to a position of good light but out of direct sunlight. Remove any glass and paper used to cover the seedtray while seeds were germinating. As soon as seedlings are large enough to handle, carefully tease them free of the compost – keeping their small, but vital, root system intact – supporting each seedling from

A vast range of seeds can be propagated in the greenhouse.

Never pick up a seedling by its fragile stem.

beneath using a dibber or pencil and steadying it by holding one seedleaf between finger and thumb. Never pick up a seedling by its fragile stem.

Depending on the size of the seedling as well as space available, transfer the seedlings either individually into pots or line them out in a seedtray.

Early in mid-spring there is still bound to be a great demand for space with many sowings still to be made and earlier sowings waiting to be hardened off. Furthermore, many other greenhouse subjects will now be demanding more and more space, particularly where early tomatoes and cucumbers are being grown.

It is still not too late to sow most of the annuals, biennials and perennials recommended for early spring. So, check through early sowings for failures because there is still time to make amends if a second batch is sown by mid-spring. Damping off fungi can be a problem, wiping out whole seedtrays of seedlings. Also, check the planned sowing programme with the seedlings now growing apace in the greenhouse. It is easy to forget to sow whole batches or mislay seed packets.

Where damping off has become a problem give each seedtray a drenching with 'Cheshunt Compound' fungicide. Also make sure all seedtrays and pots are thoroughly cleaned before re-use. Don't neglect plant hygiene with seedlings.

A second sowing of many annuals can be made later this month for use in the greenhouse and to supplement the display outside as the early sowings start to fade.

Primroses and polyanthus, that are most welcome during the dreary weeks in early spring, need to be sown now, since better germination is obtained when the seed is just ripe. Prepare a seedtray or pan of sieved peat-based seed compost and press the

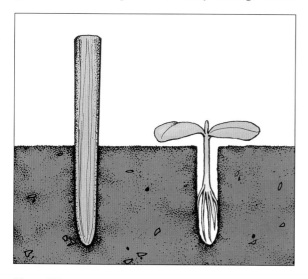

Use a dibber to make a hole in the compost, and then insert the seedling.

Polyanthus 'Crescendo'.

Zinnias will grow fast from a late spring sowing .

be made in mid-spring *Primula kewensis*, *P. obconica* (poisonous), *P. sinensis* and *P. malacoides* are all worth trying. Sow in the same manner as primroses and polyanthus for a colourful display in the winter.

Zinnias need to be sown in spring in a temperature of at least 61°F (16°C), but preferably a temperature around 64–70°F (18–21°C). They greatly resent root disturbance so they will require to be pricked out with great care into modular seedtrays. Plants can later be potted on into 3½in (9cm) pots without upsetting their sensitive root system. Harden off young plants in late spring for planting out a few weeks later.

For a kaleidoscope of winter colour, sow cinerarias in late spring. These pot plants are covered in tight clusters of flowers held clear of a compact backdrop of foliage. Sow seed thinly on seedtrays filled with sowing compost and cover lightly with

surface quite flat, leaving no holes or bumps. Water compost by standing the container in water, then allow it to drain thoroughly. Add dry silver sand to the seed packet and mix well. This will act as a spreading agent when the dust-fine seed is sown. Scatter the sand/seed mix thinly over the surface of the compost, then lightly dust them with more silver sand. Place a sheet of glass and a newspaper over the seedtray to keep the seed moist. Maintain a temperature of 61°F (16°C) in a shaded position until the first seeds have germinated. Sowings of several greenhouse primulas to be grown as pot plants can

DIVISION

Border dahlia tubers not used to produce cuttings can be increased by division in early to mid-spring. Check that the tubers are healthy before placing them in boxes containing a moist peat and sand mix. Make sure their crowns are not buried. Keep in a cool, light place to encourage dormant buds to swell.

Using a sharp knife, cut the crown into good-sized sections each with healthy tubers and a cluster of plump buds. Dust the cut sections with a fungicide such as 'flowers of sulphur' to prevent rotting. Plant out when conditions are suitable.

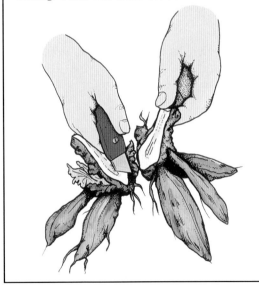

CUTTINGS

Softwood cuttings of several greenhouse plants such as fuchsias and pelargoniums can be taken in early spring. The number taken will depend on how many losses were incurred during the long, freezing winter months. All new shoots can be used, but wait until the cuttings are at least 2in (5cm) for pelargoniums and 1½in (3.75cm) for fuchsias.

Continue to take cuttings of both chrysanthemums and dahlias as suitable shoot growth becomes available. Don't make the mistake of taking ten times the number of cuttings from one variety simply because it readily produces that many more shoots, otherwise the eventual display will look rather unbalanced.

If earlier cuttings have failed or if there is a need for something to fill a colour gap in mid- to late summer then it is still possible to take cuttings of plants like salvias, geraniums and fuchsias by mid-spring. Where the failure has been caused by a disease then this must be cleared up before new cuttings are taken.

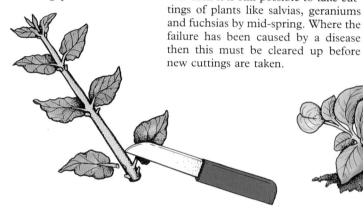

Remove leaves from the base of a fuchsia softwood cutting and insert in moist cuttings compost in a seedtray or pot.

Cover with polythene and, when rooted, pot on into individual 3in (7.5cm) pots.

compost. Maintain a temperature of around 55°F (13°C) – not usually a problem at this time of the year. Check seedtrays daily for the first signs of germination, then move them to a well-lit position out of direct sunlight. To get continuity of colour from mid-winter to late spring, several sowings must be made at intervals until mid-summer.

Vegetables

Many crops that are required throughout the summer will need to be sown in small batches several times in succession through the spring. The belief that it is possible to sow only once, grow the most vigorous seedlings on quickly and get a succession by delaying pricking out and the potting of others is mistaken. Any plant given a poor start or checked by delays will never perform well later in the sea-son. It is far better to plan out a succession of sowings every couple of weeks or so, pricking out, and potting on when the seedlings are ready.

Radish and lettuce are a good example. Earliest sowings made this year continue on from those made at the end of last and should be repeated at fortnightly intervals through mid-winter and early spring. The most vigorous seedlings should then be selected to provide a succession of delicious early salad vegetables while they're so expensive in the shops. Sowings can be made now in unheated greenhouses or cold frames and by the end of the month they can be made direct under cloches outside.

A further sowing of many vegetables sown in early spring is a good idea to maintain continuity of supply. By early spring it is possible to make sowings in a cool greenhouse – with a little bottom heat

– whereas sowings made earlier in the year required a heated greenhouse. Sow into deep seedtrays for planting out when the weather conditions allow.

Summer cabbage and cauliflowers can be sown in early spring. Cauliflowers, in particular, are prone to fail if given a check in growth during the early stages. Therefore, sow direct into modular seedtrays to reduce root disturbance when they are planted out into the vegetable plot. There are many varieties to choose from but some of the most reliable include cabbage varieties such as 'Hispi', 'Derby Day' and 'Spitfire', and cauliflowers such as 'All the Year Round' and 'Dok'.

To get a winter supply of celery you'll need to sow in early spring. A little bottom heat is needed, but this can be provided quite well in a cool greenhouse. Sow in seedtrays in the usual manner providing a temperature of around 61°F (16°C). When the seedlings are large enough, prick them out carefully in rows into deep seedtrays at least 2in (5cm) apart with 2in (5cm) between rows. In late spring harden them off ready for planting out when the soil conditions are suitable. Suitable, self-blanching varieties include 'Celebrity' and 'Ivory Towers'.

If you would like a supply of juicy cucumbers to fill your salad bowl all summer long choose all-female varieties like 'Fenomex', 'Pepimex 69', 'Pepita' and 'Telegraph'. Sow two seeds about ½in (1.25cm) deep into a 3½in (9cm) pot, placing the flat seeds on their edge to prevent rotting. Pots can then be placed in a tray for ease of handling and covered by a sheet of glass to protect them from mice. Keep the temperature around 64°F (18°C) and seedlings will appear within a week, so the pots need to be checked every day for the first signs of life. Once germinated, take off the glass and remove the weakest seedlings from each pot. Then place the remaining seedlings in good light out of direct sun. As plants fill the container, pot them off into 5in (12.5cm) containers before being planted out.

Sow sweet peppers in a seedtray. Good varieties include 'Canape' and 'Bellboy'. Aim to maintain a temperature of around 64°F (18°C). They quickly germinate and as soon as the first true leaves appear they can be potted on singly into 3½in (9cm) containers filled with potting compost. Harden off in late spring for planting out in summer.

Aubergines (egg plants) sown in late winter can be potted on before they, too, are hardened off and planted out. It is still not too late to make a sowing if the early batch failed or was forgotten.

Sow tomato seeds individually spaced in a seedtray.

During the first couple of weeks of early spring, sow tomatoes for growing in an unheated greenhouse. Good varieties include 'Gardener's Delight' and 'Shirley'. Use a propagator to maintain a germination temperature of 64°F (18°C). Later, further sowings of tomatoes can be made, but this time for cropping outside. Try 'Gardener's Delight', 'Red Alert' or 'Tornado'. The seed is large enough to sow singly and should be spaced 2in (5cm) apart in a seedtray filled with compost. As soon as the first true leaves on each seedling start to cross over or touch their neighbours in the seedtray, prick them out individually into 3½in (9cm) pots containing a potting compost. Water and feed the plants regularly and space the pots to allow free air circulation as the plants grow. By the end of mid-spring, the plants will need hardening off to be planted out in early summer as the first truss of flowers starts to show colour.

HERBS

Herbs are normally sown direct outside in late spring, but a few half-hardy species, such as bush basil (*Ocimum minimum*) and sweet basil (*Ocimum basilicum*), will benefit from a slightly earlier sowing under a warmer environment. Sow into a half seedtray or pan filled with seed compost. Prick out seedlings when large enough to handle safely into 3½in (9cm) pots filled with a peat-based potting compost. Thyme, sage and marjoram can also be sown early.

LATE STARTERS

Melons, cucumbers and tomatoes for an unheated greenhouse or for planting outside can still be sown in mid- to late spring. The large-seeded melons and cucumbers can be sown two per pot (the weaker seedling later removed) on edge in 3½in (9cm) pots. The tomatoes should be sown at 2in (5cm) intervals along rows 2in (5cm) apart in a seedtray filled with seed compost.

Sow large melon seeds on edge
to prevent rotting.

Sweetcorn ('Candle' and 'Sunrise'), marrows and courgettes ('Early Gem', 'Ambassador'), beans ('Desiree', 'Polestar', 'Streamline') and French beans ('Masterpiece', 'Tendergreen') should also be sown now for planting outside. Sow seeds singly in 3½in (9cm) pots filled with sowing compost. Cover with ½in (1.25cm) of compost and water well. Place a sheet of glass over the pots to prevent attention from mice and maintain a temperature of about 61°F (16°C). Harden off and plant out after the threat of late frosts has gone.

Fruit

In the heated greenhouse, the first strawberry flowers will be appearing early in the season, and the temperature should be raised to 60°F (15°C). Hand pollination will be necessary, using a soft brush; or dab them with cotton wool, otherwise subsequent fruit can be misshapen through poor setting. Water as necessary from now on as fruits begin to swell, but take care not to wet the crown or developing fruits.

Any fruits not developing evenly should be removed early on to channel all the plant's energy into the good fruit. Thinning may be necessary.

As vines come into flower they will also need pollinating. Ventilate the greenhouse more freely as blooms begin to develop, to reduce the humidity. Do not spray overhead and try to keep air circulating.

Those peaches and nectarines being grown in a cool greenhouse will blossom in spring and so will need pollinating and disbudding. Those in a heated greenhouse will need watering and damping down daily after the fruits have set. Fruit thinning may well be necessary, but don't get carried away too soon since there is often a natural fruit thinning during mid-spring when many set fruit wither and drop off.

POLLINATION

Fruit such as peaches, nectarines and apricots are normally insect-pollinated but in the greenhouse this is a far from reliable method so some form of assistance must be given.

Using a soft paintbrush, or something similar, transfer pollen from one flower to another by gently dabbing the brush into each flower. The most effective time is just around noon when the greenhouse is warmest. During this period the greenhouse needs to be kept constantly warm to get a good set. After setting, spray the plants daily.

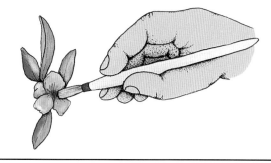

SOWING IDEAS

Name	Germ. Temp. (°C)	Germ. Time (wks)	Plant Out	Comments
ANNUALS				
Ageratum houstonianum e.g.'Adriatic', 'Blue Blazer', 'Pacific'	18–21	1–2	late spring early summer	A rather compact plant that flowers from early spring to the first frost.
Alyssum maritimum e.g. 'Snow Crystals' (white), 'Wonderland' (mixed and single colours)	10–15	1–2	mid-spring	Transplant either singly or in clumps. Blooms from early summer to early autumn.
Amaranthus caudatus (love-lies-bleeding)	21–24	1–2	late spring	Sow on surface. Striking ropes of blood-red blooms up to 2ft (60cm) long.
Arctotis grandis (African daisy)	15–18	3–4	mid-spring late spring	Grey-blue centre surrounded by delicate white and pink petals – blooms during summer months.
Begonia semperflorens e.g. 'Cocktail', 'Party Fun'	18–21	2–4	late spring early summer	Sow on surface. Red, pink or white flowers produced from early summer to early autumn.
Brachycome iberidifolia (swan river daisy) e.g. 'Mixed'	18–21	1–2	late spring	Sow on surface. Pink, blue and white starry flowers are fragrant and appear from early summer until the first frost of autumn.
Callistephus chinensis (China aster) e.g. 'Colour Carpet', 'Crimson Sunset'	15–18	2–4	late spring	Daisy-like flower from mid-summer until mid-autumn in shades of red, pink, yellow and purple.
Celosia argenta plumosa e.g. 'Century Mixed'	18–21	2–3	late spring early summer	Need to be hardened off carefully before planting out. Blooms all summer long.
Cleome spinosa	18–21	2	late spring	White blooms flushed with pink from mid-summer onwards. Several good coloured varieties.
Convolvulus tricolour e.g. 'Dwarf Rainbow Flash'	15–18	1–2	late spring	Intense blue flowers with contrasting centres of yellow and white. Appear all summer.
Coreopsis tinctoria	15–18	2–4	late spring	Brilliant yellow, red and in between shades on stems. From mid-summer to early autumn.
Cosmos e.g. 'Sonata' (white), 'Sensation' (mixed)	15–18	1–2	late spring	Flower early summer to mid-autumn. Dead head to prevent self-seeding.
Dianthus chinensis e.g. 'Fire Carpet', 'Parfait' (series), 'Telstar' (mixture)	13–15	2–3	late spring	Neat, even display from early summer to the first frost.
Dimorphotheca aurantiaca (star of the Veldt)	15–21	1–2	late spring	Superb for tubs, windowboxes, baskets, walls and rockery. Blooms from early summer to early autumn in various colours.

Name	Germ. Temp. (°C)	Germ. Time (wks)	Plant Out	Comments
Gerbera jamesonii (Transvaal daisy)	18–21	2–3	late spring	Fabulously coloured large blooms on strong stems from late spring to late autumn.
Godetia e.g. 'Dwarf Mixed', 'Salmon Princess'	15–18	1–2	late spring	Brilliant show of flowers from early summer to mid-autumn.
Gomphrena globosa (bachelor's buttons) (purple), e.g. 'Buddy', 'Gnome White'	15–21	1–2	late spring	Long-lasting blooms appear from mid-summer to early autumn. Ideal pot plant.
Helianthus annus (sunflower) e.g. 'Sunburst Mixed', 'Sunbeam', 'Moonwalker'	15–18	2	late spring	Both mixed and single colour varieties around 4–5ft tall.
Hibiscus trionum (flower-of-an-hour) e.g. 'Sunnyday'	15–18	1–2	late spring	2in (5cm) blooms in pale yellow with a purple centre. Flowers all summer long.
Impatiens (busy Lizzies) e.g. 'Accent', 'Super Elfin' (both mixed and single colours)	18–21	3–4	late spring early summer	Suitable for growing in pots under glass. Blooms in a range of colours produced from early summer to early autumn.
Ipomoea purpurea	18–21	1–3	late spring early summer	Richly coloured blooms 2in (5cm) across all summer.
Ipomoea tricolour (morning glory) e.g. 'Heavenly Blue'	18–21	1–3	late spring early summer	Produces early blooms in stunning sky-blue.
Kochia scoparia trichophylla (burning bush)	15–21	1–2	late spring	Much underrated plant that produces a clean pale green mound of foliage that gradually turns deep red.
Lychnis coronaria alba	18–21	2–3	late spring	Superb plant for silver and whiteborder. Grey hairy foliage and white flowers produced from mid-summer to early autumn.
Matthiola bicornis (night scented stock)	15–18	2	mid-spring late spring	Rather dull lilac blooms on spikes between mid- to late summer. At night they open to produce a heady scent.
Matthiola incana (East Lothian stocks) e.g. 'Mixed'	15–18	1–2	mid-spring late spring	Flowers appear in early to mid-summer on 12in (30cm) spikes in a range of colours from white to purple.
Moluccella laevis (shellflower)	15–21	2–3	late spring	Spikes of white fragrant flowers each surrounded by a shell-like green calyx.
Nemesia strumosa e.g. 'Carnival Mixed', 'Brown's Fairy Lights', 'Suttons Sparkler'	15–18	2	late spring	Funnel-shaped blooms in a range of colours produced from early to late summer. Look best when planted close together in a group.

Name	Germ. Temp. (°C)	Germ. Time (wks)	Plant Out	Comments
Nicotiana alata (tobacco plant)	18–21	2–3	late spring	Blooms from mid-summer to early autumn producing a sweet scent. Grow in shade if you want to see flowers open during the day.
Phlox drummondii e.g. 'Beauty Mixed', 'Phlox of Sheep' (pastel)	15–18	2–3	late spring	From mid-summer to early autumn blooms in varying shades.
Reseda odorata (mignonette)	13–15	1–2	late spring	Small ¼in (6mm) blooms are produced all summer long in yellow or orange.
Tagetes (Afro-French) e.g. 'Solar' series, 'Super Star' series	18–21	1–2	late spring	Cross between African and French Marigolds. Produce compact, bushy plants with single or double blooms.
Tagetes erecta (African marigold) e.g. 'Galore Mixed', 'Luxor Mixed'	18–21	1–2	late spring	Dark green leaves set off the scented yellow blooms produced from mid-summer until the first frost.
Tagetes patula (French Marigold) e.g. 'Sajan Tangerine', 'Silva'	18–21	1–2	late spring	Deep orange and yellow blooms 2in (5cm) across. Produced all summer long.
Tagetes tenuifolia (marigold) e.g. 'Lemon Gem', 'Tangerine Gem'	18–21	1–2	late spring	Bright flowers 1in (2.5cm) across produced from mid-summer to early autumn.
Thunbergia alata (black-eyed Susan)	15–21	2–3	late spring early summer	2in (5cm) wide flowers are produced from mid-summer onwards. Orange petals with purple central tube.
Zinnia elegans	18–21	1–2	late spring early summer	Produces blooms from mid-summer to early autumn in a range of colours from white to red.

PERENNIALS:

Name	Germ. Temp. (°C)	Germ. Time (wks)	Plant Out	Comments
Alstroemeria ligtu (Peruvian lily)	18–21	4–5	early summer	Pink and orange blooms in early to mid-summer. A half-hardy species that grows to about 24in (60cm).
Alyssum saxatile e.g. 'Golden Queen'	15–18	2	late spring	Ground-hugging plant with grey foliage covered in masses of yellow blooms in spring.
Antirrhinum majus (snapdragon)	16–18	2–3	mid-spring early summer	Light is necessary for germination. Flowers from mid-summer to early autumn in a variety of colours.
Calceolaria Hyb. e.g. 'Anytime Series'	18–21	2–3	potgrown	Sow on the surface to get a show four months later. Various colours.
Canna (Indian shot)	21–24	3–8	late spring	Soak seed 24hrs before sowing. Colours: scarlet, pink, orange, salmon and yellow. Bloom from mid-summer to early autumn.

Name	Germ. Temp. (°C)	Germ. Time (wks)	Plant Out	Comments
Catananche caerulea (Cupid's dart)	13–15	2–3	late spring	Summer flowers of brilliant sky-blue.
Heliotropium e.g. 'Dwarf Marine'	18–21	1–4	late spring	Large fragrant, purple flowers produced all summer. Deep green foliage. Can be used as bedding or in pots.
Mesembryanthemum criniflorum (livingstone daisy) e.g. 'Magic Carpet Mixed'	15–18	2–3	late spring	Starry flowers in a variety of colours that are produced through the summer. Prefers a sunny spot.
Petunia e.g. 'Carpet Series Mixed', 'Cascade' (series)	15–18	2–3	late spring early summer	Wide range of varieties that produce fabulous display all summer. Select smallest seedlings because they produce the best colours.
Salvia patens	18–21	2–3	late spring	Provides a late summer to early autumn display of azure blue claw-shaped flowers.
Salvia splendens	18–21	2–3	late spring	Best known as summer bedding with its easily recognizable blazing red flower spike. From mid-summer to early autumn.
Sinningia speciosa (gloxinia)	18–24	2–4	potgrown	Sow on surface. Beautiful display from late spring to late summer with spectacular blooms in a range of colours.
Tropaeolum peregrinum (canary creeper)	13–18	2	mid-spring late spring	Fast-growing creeper that produces lots of pretty yellow flowers all summer.
Verbena × hybrida	18–21	3–4	late spring	Many varieties available giving a wide range of sparkling colours from early summer to early autumn.

PLANTING

Flowers

For a profusion of magnificent blooms in a rainbow of colours from late spring to late autumn start tuberous begonias into growth now. Select only firm, healthy tubers and place them in trays filled with moist peat, hollow side facing upwards. If the temperature is kept around the 64°F (18°C) mark then plump buds will soon swell ready for moving on either individually into 6in (15cm) pots or several planted into large containers. Pendulous varieties like 'Pendula Chanson Mixed' with its semi-double blossoms of copper, scarlet, crimson, white and yellow, or the cascading 'Illuminated Pink Salmon', which has double blooms, are ideal for planting in a hanging basket or tub to get a waterfall of colours.

Stunning cannas add an exotic touch to borders during the summer and can be started now in pots in the greenhouse. Plant fleshy root sections in 3½in (9cm) pots filled with a peat-based potting compost. Water well and aim to maintain a temperature of about 59°F (15°C).

Achimenes can still be started into growth at a temperature of about 61°F (16°C). Fill a 5in (12.5cm) pot with a peat-based potting compost and space six to eight grub-like tubers over the surface. For a really stunning display try planting achimenes in a hanging basket to produce a cascade of pure white, red or pink all summer long.

To maintain a succession of eye-catching blooms, a batch of hippeastrum bulbs can be delayed by not planting them until mid-spring. Pot a single bulb into a 5in (12.5cm) container filled with potting compost. Water sparingly until signs of growth appear, then water more freely as the flowerbud pushes upwards. Feeding is important from this point on and must be continued after the flower has faded until the leaves start to turn yellow. Then stop feeding and reduce watering slowly to nothing to allow the plant to go into its dormancy period.

Earlier chrysanthemum cuttings – those taken during early spring – and potted on for planting out of doors will be ready for hardening off in a cold frame. If there is no space available there then by the end of the month it will be safe to place them in the shelter of a south-west facing wall protected on cold nights with a layer of horticultural fleece.

Once hardened off they are ready to be planted out in their flowering position. Select a sheltered site and prepare it by digging in well-rotted farmyard manure to a well-dug plot. Where quite a number are to be grown for cut flowers, say, mark out a bed 4ft (1.2m) wide and put a stout post in each corner. Then lay a sheet of 5in (12.5cm) mesh pea and bean netting over the bed, attaching it to a wooden crossbar at each end with a length of strong wire woven through each side of the netting and running from one crossbar to the other. Fix the wire securely to the crossbars so the netting is held out flat. Place one crossbar over the posts at one end and then using the other crossbar roll the wire and netting up until, when pulled really taut it can be slipped tightly onto the two posts at the other end of the bed. Push both crossbars down to ground level.

Plant shallowly in three staggered rows. Then, as the plants grow and develop, slip the crossbars up the posts to support them. Water after planting and water and feed regularly from next month onwards. If, however, only a few chrysanthemums are to be grown then they can be placed in the borders or as a single row and supported individually with a stout bamboo cane.

Hardy perennials raised from seed or cuttings will be ready for planting out into the garden in late

BEDDING

The clearing of beds and borders for bedding should be carried out in late spring to take the pressure off greenhouse and frame space as quickly as possible. Already bedding plants will be being hardened off in the upper reaches of the greenhouse or in the cold frame. Before summer begins, nearly all will be planted out in the garden and growing away.

With bedding being moved out, areas of greenhouse staging will start to be cleared ready for the potted seedlings and rooted cuttings from last month. Where temporary staging becomes redundant later in late spring, take it down to make way for the space-hungry summer crops of tomatoes, cucumbers and melons.

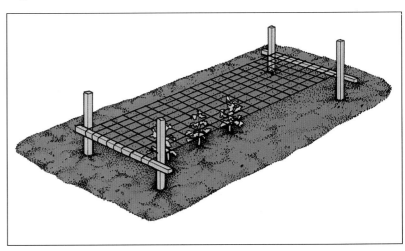

Plant chrysanthemums in staggered rows under mesh.

COLD FRAMES

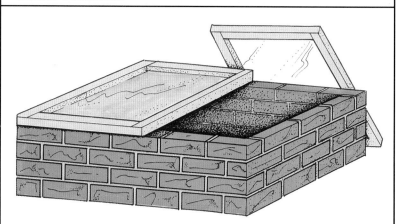

A cold frame consisting of brick walls and detachable lights is ideal, but if space is a problem you can make a cloche by fastening together two panes of glass with a special clip, which will provide some protection for plants.

spring once hardened off. Alpines, too, can be set out.

Successful Hanging Baskets

Beautiful hanging baskets are easy to create: use the plant lists included in this section to choose the right plants for your situation and then follow the step-by-step guide overleaf for perfect baskets every time.

Fuchsias can be planted up in hanging baskets. If done now the plants will have plenty of time to settle in and may well be in flower when they go outside. Line the basket with moss and place an old saucer in its base to help retention of moisture. Fill the lined basket with potting compost and plant three or four fuchsias in a 14in (35cm) diameter basket. Once the plants are established pinch out the growing tips to encourage bushiness.

Remember that as the season progresses, hanging baskets will need watering more frequently as the plants become established and begin to grow away.

Geranium 'Summer showers' is a good basket subject.

PLANTING A BASKET STEP-BY-STEP

MATERIALS

❀ **Basket** Large baskets are best (at least 14in diameter). They hold much more compost and so can accommodate a better display of plants and hold more water: 12in basket holds 6 litres of compost; 14in 11 litres of compost; and 16in 17 litres of compost.

❀ **Chain** Check it is in good condition.

❀ **Bracket** Needs to be strong to take the weight and must be attached securely. Check welds before you buy.

❀ **Liner** The choice of materials is growing fast. Apart from traditional sphagnum moss, you can now find liners made from coconut fibre, coir or foam. Perhaps you would like to try something a bit different such as capillary matting, plastic mesh or even clippings from a conifer hedge.

❀ **Compost** Fresh, good quality.

❀ **Fertilizer pellets** Use slow-release fertilizer pellets.

1. Stand the empty basket on a bucket or empty pot, so that it is stable.

2. Line the basket. If you are using moss, cover the bottom of the basket with about 1in thick of moss.

3. Lay a piece of polythene (the bag the moss came in for instance) or old saucer on top of the moss to help retain moisture in the compost.

4. Fill the bottom of the basket with good compost.

5. Plant trailing plants through the mesh about half way up the side. Always push the shoots through from the inside rather than the rootball through from the outside to avoid damaging the root system. To make this easier, wrap the shoots tightly in paper before trying to push them through the mesh.

6. Pack extra moss around the base of the shoots to prevent compost falling out of the basket.

7. Fill the basket with more compost and then add slow-release fertilizer pellets (the number will depend on the size of your basket).

8. Plant the large central plant in the top first then the mix of bushy and trailing plants around the edges.

9. Top up with compost and firm.

10. Insert the empty 3in pot rim-deep into the compost near the centre where it will not be seen. This will make watering easier through the summer months by preventing the water running straight off the basket.

POSITIONING YOUR BASKET

❀ Keep it in a frost-free place until it is safe to position outside. Alternatively, put the basket outside and bring it in only when cold weather threatens (in practise this means most nights and some days, especially windy ones).

❀ Put up the bracket in an open position. Avoid very hot spots but the basket will do best if it is in a sunny position for most of the day (south-east or south-west facing walls are often best).

❀ Avoid areas where the basket will get buffeted by winds, such as between buildings where wind is funnelled.

AFTERCARE

❀ Keep the basket well watered. In practice this means watering every evening even in wet weather because precious little water will soak into the compost.

❀ If no slow-release fertilizer pellets were added at planting time, feed once a week with a high-potash liquid feed to encourage flowering or a balanced liquid feed to encourage flowers and foliage.

❀ To get an even shape, turn the basket once a week so that all plants get equal amounts of light.

❀ Preen the basket regularly to remove fading flowers and yellowing leaves.

❀ Check for outbreaks of pests and diseases every time you water.

FLOWERING PLANTS

Ageratum	Lobelia
Alyssum	Osteospermum
Begonia (fibrous rooted)	Marigolds: African
Begonia (tuberous)	Afro-French
Bellis	French
Bidens ferulifoli	Mimulus
Brachycome multiflora	Nasturtium
Calceolaria	Nemisia
Campanula isophyll	Pansy
Coleus	Pelargoniums
Convolvulus sabatius	(trailing and ivy leaved)
Dianthus	Petunia
Diascia integrimma	Portulaca
Felicia	Tagetes
Fuchsias (cascading)	Thunbergia alata
Gazania	Tropaeolum
Heliotrope	Verbena
Impatiens	Viola

FOLIAGE PLANTS

Ajuga	Lysimachia
Cineraria maritima	Nepeta
Euonymus fortunei	Plectranthus
Helichrysum petiolare	Parsley
Ivy	Spider plant
Lamium	Tomato 'Tumbler'
Lotus berthelotii	Tradescantia

Vegetables and Fruit

Cucumbers sown in late winter will be large enough to plant out in early spring in a heated greenhouse. The simplest method is to grow two or three plants in a growing bag. However, cucumbers can also be grown in the border soil. Prepare a bed in the greenhouse border early in the month by digging in plenty of well-rotted manure. Then build up a ridge of compost made from quality garden loam (sterilized) and well-rotted compost in a half-and-half mix. The ridge will need to be at least 18in (45cm) high and 2ft (60cm) long for every plant grown. Four or five plants will keep an average family self-sufficient in cucumbers throughout the summer.

Raise the temperature to at least 64°F (18°C) before planting. When the young cucumbers are 6in (15cm) tall place them 2ft (60cm) apart along the ridge, providing each with a cane for initial support. Lightly firm and water well.

Young cucumber plants sown early in spring should be planted into cool or unheated greenhouses by the end of mid-spring. Prepare the bed in the same manner as described for early cucumbers (below).

It is time to plant tomatoes when the majority of the plants are showing colour in the first truss of flowers. Tomatoes should be set out 18in (45cm) apart in the border and spaced equally in a growing bag – the number per bag will depend on the volume of compost it contains. Aim for a temperature around 50°F (10°C) at night, rising to between 61°F (16°C) and 64°F (18°C) during the day.

Ventilation should be given when necessary to keep the temperature down on warm, still spring days. At night, leave a top vent open when the weather is particularly mild.

Tomatoes set out in an unheated greenhouse in mid-spring could well be looking a bit blue after a few cold nights. Protect plants with layers of horticultural fleece at night until chilly spells end.

Tomatoes sown in mid-winter will now be growing rapidly and will need spacing out on the staging to prevent a check in growth or drawn plants. Plant out into border or growing bag when colour can be seen on the first truss of each plant.

Plant tomato plants in growing bags in late spring.

Hand pollination isn't always necessary but for a good set on the first truss it's worth visiting each flower systematically with a soft paintbrush. This should be done on warm days before midday.

Harden off sweet peppers and aubergines that have established themselves in 3½in (9cm) pots. Plant out in late spring in milder areas and you will need to support each plant with a bamboo cane. Plants being grown under glass should be potted on or planted into a growing bag – two or three plants per bag is usual depending on volume.

STARTING VINES

For grape vines grown in an unheated house it is now time to start them into growth. Do this by closing the vents and increasing day and night temperature. Dormant buds will then begin to swell and break by the end of the month. Untie the vine's stems (rods) from their supporting wires and bend them over so that the tips are just off the ground. The rising sap will then not rush straight to the terminal bud – encouraging even shoot development down the stem rather than leading shoots breaking away vigorously. Water thoroughly and damp down each day.

Those vines in heated greenhouses will have already started and the stage they have reached will depend on when the greenhouse was closed down as well as the subsequent temperatures and humidity.

Peppers are as easy to grow in growing bags as tomatoes.

Cauliflowers sown in the autumn need to be hardened off ready for planting out as soon as conditions allow. It is most important not to check the growth of these plants because this can cause them to 'button' later on. That is, the curd will not develop beyond a button-sized inflorescence. Therefore, lift plants with the utmost care with all roots intact. If you sow in modular seedtrays or peat pots this problem is largely avoided.

When healthy melons have developed their fifth leaf they are ready to be planted either into a prepared bed or a growing bag. Bring the growing bag into the greenhouse a few days before planting up so it can warm in the spring sunshine. Securely fasten several wires about 12in (30cm) apart to the greenhouse frame to provide support. Plant up the melons and stick a sturdy cane by each, tying the tops of the canes to the first wire.

POTTING AND REPOTTING

Rooted cuttings of perpetual-flowering carnations, pelargoniums, fuchsias, coleus and the like, will need to be potted on when they have outgrown their 3½in (9cm) pots. Move them on into 5in (12.5cm) pots using potting compost. Water in well and return them to their shaded position on the greenhouse staging. Ventilate freely and maintain a temperature of about 59°F (15°C). Once the plants are established, pinch out growing tips to encourage bushiness. Then harden off any plants destined for the great outdoors. Any plant material removed when stopping can be trimmed up just below a node, lower leaves removed and inserted into a gritty compost as cuttings. Rooting is quick at this time of year so that these cuttings may well require potting up individually in 3½in (9cm) pots next month.

Chrysanthemums to be grown in the greenhouse in late summer will need to be potted on into 5in (12.5cm) pots as they fill their 3½in (9cm) containers. During

REPOTTING A PLANT STEP-BY-STEP

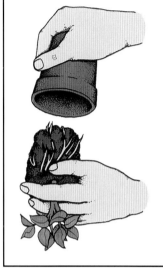

1. Water plants thoroughly, then leave for an hour or two before re-potting. Remove any loose compost from around the rootball by gently rubbing it with your hand.

2. Select a pot slightly larger than the first.

3. Cover the base with a layer of peat-based potting compost and stand the plant in the centre to check the planting level is at least ½in (1cm) below the rim.

4. Tip new compost around the rootball, firming as you go to remove air pockets.

5. Top up with compost so there is a fine covering of the rootball. Firm lightly and water.

the summer they will need potting on again into 8in (20cm) pots and placed in a sheltered spot in the garden to enjoy the warmest weather. For each repotting it is best to use loam-based compost such as J.I.P. No. 3 which will provide a stable base.

Many house and greenhouse pot plants will require repotting at this time of year. The repotting process is straightforward enough, but deciding whether a particular plant needs moving into a larger pot is not so easy. If an actively growing, healthy plant is potted on too early it can do more damage than if left to get a little pot bound. The answer is to err on the side of caution.

Once a plant appears to have filled its pot, knock it out and check the root system. If the roots have not completely filled the compost then leave, but where roots have started curling around the bottom it's time to repot.

WATERING, FEEDING, HEAT AND SHADE

Melons need to be watered with care since these plants suffer from rotting around the base of the stem. For this reason many gardeners sink an empty plant pot into the border compost about 6in (15cm) away from the melon plant and fill this several times each watering. This system also ensures that water gets deep into the border compost. Later in the season they still require a warm humid atmosphere and so damping down must be done with great care. They also require shading from the sunniest weather. Water and feed regularly.

All tomatoes will be growing rapidly, so special attention should be paid to their water requirements. Don't let the temperature get too high either, since lanky growth is of little use.

Having said this, cucumbers require a high temperature – at least 70°F (21°C) at night. Ventilation should be shut down most of the time to maintain this temperature, only being opened on very warm days. Always shut vents before nightfall to capture the warm solar-heated air inside the greenhouse.

Since cucumbers require such warm and humid conditions they don't fit in with the growing of tomatoes that like it drier and more airy. However, it is quite possible to grow them side by side if you are prepared to compromise your growing technique.

With the increased power of the sun, new vine growth can suffer from scorch, so light shading should be provided. Small greenhouses are most vulnerable because they warm up most quickly. Either apply a proprietary shading whitewash to the glass, or hang up a shading fabric or blind.

Peaches and nectarines will be swelling rapidly by late spring. They should be watered thoroughly and damped down daily once the fruits have set. Take care when cultivating soil under peaches and nectarines because their surface roots resent disturbance of any kind. Thin fruit if this has not already been done (*see* 'Training and Thinning' below). The earliest started trees will have ripening fruit this month when damping down must be stopped.

Raise the temperature for strawberries when fruit has set to around 68°F (20°C) during the day and 59°F (15°C) at night. Continue to water and feed plants as necessary.

TRAINING AND THINNING

Flowers

Fuchsias being trained as standards will need their sideshoots pinched out after the first pair of leaves.

Bush-grown fuchsias should be pinched out to encourage vigorous, bushy growth.

When the fuchsia standard has reached the height required, pinch out the growing tip to prevent further upward growth and to cause the sideshoots to develop.

The tips of sideshoots should then be pinched out a couple of times to encourage a bushy head.

The leading shoot should be kept straight by using a bamboo cane and ties. Once at the required height, pinch the leading shoot out and allow the next six or seven sideshoots to develop to form the head.

When the plants have reached the desired height, pinch out the growing tip and the tips of the top six shoots, forming the head. Repeat the process to produce a compact well-balanced head. Fuchsias grown in pots and baskets will need pinching out to encourage a bushy well-structured plant.

Early carnations and chrysanthemum cuttings will have rooted and started putting on growth rapidly. When they reach about 4in (10cm) high and have put on six or seven leaves it is time to pinch them out. Take them back to about 3in (7.5cm), removing one or two leaf joints. Do this by holding the plant firmly between finger and thumb at the desired leaf joint, then move the growing tip sharply from one side to the other. The top will break out cleanly. This action encourages the development of basal sideshoots, producing a sturdier, bushy plant.

Plants stopped in this way will produce a lush crop of sideshoots as the season progresses. Where more than three or four breaks have shot up, then the weakest should be pinched out as soon as possible.

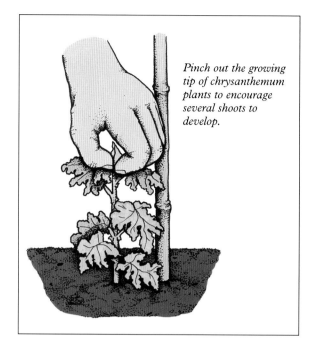

Pinch out the growing tip of chrysanthemum plants to encourage several shoots to develop.

However, where prizes at the local horticultural show are the aim then restrict these breaks to two per plant.

Vegetables and Fruit

Tomato plants develop quickly in the long, warm days of spring and soon some form of training will need to be adopted if they are not to get out of hand. A couple of weeks after planting they will

Plant sweetpeas out in late spring and provide support with stakes and large-mesh netting.

need extra support. This can be given in two ways; either tie them up to individual canes; or attach them to an overhead wire with a length of string.

Ties should be every 6in (15cm) or so up the stem and must be secure without being constricting – remember the tomato stem will swell at the base as the plant grows. Tie the top of the cane to an overhead wire for stability. Where growing bags are being used, then it might be necessary to invest in one of the specially designed support systems that uses the weight of the bag to give the crop a steady support.

String training can be used for tomatoes grown in border soil or growing bags. It is simply a matter of having one end looped securely around the base of the plant – again with plenty of room in the loop – while the other end is tied to an overhead wire using a secure slip knot. As the tomato plant grows the string is carefully wound around the stem in a spiral. One complete revolution every 6in (15cm) or so, is enough to give overall support. This training can usually be done without untying the slip knot on the overhead wire – simply manoeuvring the growth around the string. However, where growth has exceeded expectations then the slip knot can be carefully slackened, the plant trained and the knot retightened again.

For long season (early) tomatoes this system could not take account of the height of the tomato plant after several months of growth – perhaps as much as 12ft (4m). In these circumstances another string training system is required. This involves having a piece of string long enough to take account of so much growth (12ft/4m long), then attaching one end to the tomato plant as before and the other to a special S-hook (available from specialist suppliers). The excess string at the beginning of the season is wound around this S-hook until all the slack is taken up. The S-hook is then hung over the overhead wire. The training of the tomato plant early in the season is exactly the same as before, but when the plant reaches the overhead wire a little string (about 1ft/30cm) is unwound from the S-hook and the hook returned to the overhead wire about 6in (15cm) to one side. This causes the tomato plant to lean to one side. Repeat this several times and the plant stem is slowly layered. Keep the stem off the ground by tying it to a low-level wire.

After the plant has been trained it is time to remove all sideshoots. Don't do this before training just in case there is an accident and the growing point is broken out – if this happens before sideshooting, then the most vigorous sideshoot can be trained up instead of the broken growing point. Remove sideshoots by pinching the soft growth between forefinger and thumb. Bush varieties and the trailing variety 'Tumbler' should be left to their own devices.

Once settled, the melons grow away quickly and will need training. Tie the main leader to the cane guiding it to the first wire. Pinch out the leading shoot just above the last wire and tie in lateral shoots to the horizontal wires. These should then be pinched out when they've developed their fifth leaf. Throughout this period of rapid growth the plant will benefit from a humid atmosphere, so regular damping down of leaves and floor are worthwhile. Provide a little shading on very warm, sunny days.

When the new shoots on grape vines reach 18in (45cm) long, many will have produced flower trusses. Let the shoot develop until two leaves have unfolded beyond the truss and then pinch it out. Those without flower trusses will also need pinching out.

Early starters will have passed this stage earlier in the spring and, with luck, be showing fruits of previous labours. These fruits will need thinning so that they have a chance of developing into something usable. Water and feed as required. Aim to leave at least one good-sized bunch of fruit per 1ft (30cm) run of wire. The first step is to remove weaker trusses in close proximity to other better developed bunches. Also discard those trusses in a poor position; those next to the glass, as well as those that are too high, too low or just awkward to get at.

Once this is done turn to the bunches remaining to shape and thin them. To thin grapes with ease it is necessary to have the right tools. A specialist pair of grape-thinning scissors are best, but any sharp, pointed, small yet sturdy snips or scissors will do. A short prop (stick with a forked tip) is also useful to support and separate the bunches that are being thinned. It is important to avoid touching the grapes at all costs because handling destroys the fruits' bloom – the dusty white covering to each grape – and will thus weaken their natural defences.

Many early peaches will have rapidly swelling fruits. If good-sized fruits are required then some judicious thinning will probably be necessary. Pick off misshapen or stunted fruitlets. Then remove awkwardly growing fruits – those pressed against stems, wires or the greenhouse structure. Thin slowly over a period of weeks to get best results. Stop when there are about two fruits per square foot of vertical area covered by the tree.

RESTING

Several precious winter and early spring-flowering greenhouse plants will now be coming to the end of their season. Freesias, for instance, will need resting during the early summer months for them to perform the following winter. Water well while the plants remain in flower, but reduce this slowly to nothing as they begin to die down. Water occasionally thereafter to prevent the compost from becoming dust dry.

Many bulbous plants like nerines, lachenalias, arum lilies and cyclamen also need a restful summer. Again, slowly reduce watering after the last flowers fade, allowing the leaves to yellow and die back naturally. The bulbs should be left in the dry compost and pot until they are started off into growth again during late summer. Store arum lilies on their sides under staging away from drips, but leave nerines and lachenalias in a sunny spot where they can ripen.

Thin peaches by removing the smallest fruit.

CHAPTER 7

Summer

GENERAL MANAGEMENT

Early Summer

The threat of night frosts is over in many areas by the beginning of early summer. In exceptional years, though, they can catch out the unwary gardener by appearing as late as this time of year. In colder climes, of course, freezing night temperatures can be a reality even later in the year.

The long sunny days will cause the temperature in the greenhouse to rise rapidly in the mornings and stay hot all day. Rapid rises in temperature, and falls for that matter, should be avoided by careful ventilation early in the morning as well as later afternoon. Where an automatic vent opener is on the shopping list, it would be worthwhile buying it now so that it can be fitted before the ventilator has become less accessible.

There will of course, be the added benefit of having an automatic vent throughout the summer. Furthermore, if mid-summer is hot then the stock of automatic vents on sale will be in short supply as demand rises.

**EARLY SUMMER
QUICK REFERENCE CHECKLIST**

* Keep a check on temperatures by regulating the ventilation.
* Put up shading where necessary.
* Check watering requirements daily.

FLOWERS

* Sow *Primula malacoides*, *P. sinensis* and *P. kewensis*.
* Sow cinerarias and alpine calceolarias.
* Take softwood cuttings.
* Pot on rooted cuttings as necessary.

VEGETABLES

* Train tomatoes and cucumbers.
* Sideshoot tomatoes.
* Water and feed carefully.
* Harden off aubergines, sweet peppers, marrows and ridge cucumbers.

FRUIT

* Thin grapes.
* Water and feed peaches, nectarines and strawberries.

Sow stocks in mid-summer.

Pot lily.

Hot days will require free ventilation both top and bottom. Extra ventilation can be gained by opening the door or, in extreme cases, removing one or two panes of glass.

Shading will be necessary in early summer for many greenhouse plants. Either apply a proprietary shading whitewash designed to be painted directly onto the outside of the glass or put up a shading fabric if not already done. This can be anything from a cheap plastic mesh to the more expensive blinds. Blinds, of course, are preferable because they can be rolled up or down as the need arises.

Watering is by now the most time-consuming job in the greenhouse especially for tomatoes, cucumbers, melons and fruit trees. Hours can be spent each day checking and watering each plant. In addition, some crops such as tomatoes suffer when they become water stressed – encouraging problems like blossom end rot that render whole trusses of fruit useless.

Feeding once a fortnight will be required by most plants in the active growth phase. Select a high-potash fertilizer for fruiting and flowering crops – a tomato fertilizer is ideal. For leafy plants choose something with a balance of the nutrients nitrogen, phosphorus and potassium (NPK).

Mid-summer

The greenhouse in mid-summer is a hot and humid place with a mixture of flowers and vegetables coming into their main season. Greenhouse climbers such as bougainvilleas, *Plumbago capensis*, lapagerias and the ever-popular passion flower are all blooming profusely this month.

Keeping the greenhouse cool enough is the main problem in mid-summer. Opening vents both top and bottom as well as leaving the door open is often not enough on those hot, still, balmy days. Removing glass panes, as described in early summer is a laborious job that nobody wants to do and on still days this has very little beneficial effect.

Forced ventilation is the only real answer – some form of extractor fan built into the end wall of the greenhouse to push hot air out and draw cool air in. Air movement is important because it will reduce the incidence of disease.

Keep a close check on the temperature in your greenhouse, particularly if it is small and heats up

---

MID-SUMMER
QUICK REFERENCE CHECKLIST

❀ Careful ventilation is essential to control greenhouse temperatures.
❀ Put up permanent shading.
❀ Water as and when necessary.
❀ Check for pests and diseases.
❀ Send heaters off to be serviced.

FLOWERS

❀ Sow cinerarias and alpine calceolarias.
❀ Sow stocks and mignonette (*Reseda odorata*).
❀ Prick out primulas and other seedlings.
❀ Take cuttings of *Hydrangea petiolaris*, abelia, forsythia and many other garden shrubs.

VEGETABLES

❀ Water and feed plants as necessary.
❀ Train tomatoes, cucumbers and melons.
❀ Check for pests and diseases.

FRUIT

❀ Thin grapes.
❀ Feed and water all fruit.
❀ Harvest ripe fruit.
❀ Check strawberry plants for greenfly.
❀ Select strawberry runners for forcing next year.

PESTS AND DISEASES

Pests and diseases will be eager to take over the greenhouse and its bounty of crops if you are not careful. So check all the plants thoroughly as often as possible for any signs of damage or pest and disease presence. Spider mite, thrips, whitefly and greenfly continue to be a nuisance and caterpillars may well put in an appearance. Placing a net over ventilators to keep out butterflies will eliminate the caterpillar problem, but make certain the net doesn't foul the workings of the vent.

quickly. Here a maximum/minimum thermometer is a good investment and will indicate when the greenhouse precautions against the sun are working. More shading is often required mid-summer with even sun-lovers like tomatoes needing protection. Check the shading material you have already erected to see that it is intact or; if you have used the whitewash type, not wearing thin or flaking off.

A watering routine will now be well under way, so little extra has to be added. But don't become complacent because plants will soon suffer if they run short of water – reducing yield and developing other associated problems. Check each plant at least once a day, but on hot days two or even three waterings will be necessary for those plants with limited root run. Feeding at fortnightly intervals should also be continued to keep actively growing plants happy. Hungry plants such as tomatoes require feeding every week.

Heaters will become completely redundant this month and can be removed from the greenhouse. Don't just throw them in a corner of the potting shed for the summer but give them a thorough overhaul. Check for faults, sending machines away for any repairs so that they are ready for use in the greenhouse by the end of early autumn.

Late Summer

In good years or bad years, depending on your point of view, late summer can often bring many of our hottest days. When the weather doesn't break, close, hot days will persist, and this makes effective ventilation in the greenhouse difficult to achieve.

We are now well into the main growing season

LATE SUMMER QUICK REFERENCE CHECKLIST

- ❀ Keep the greenhouse cool by careful shading and ventilation.
- ❀ Water carefully throughout the month.

FLOWERS

- ❀ Prick out sowings made last month.
- ❀ Sow schizanthus and *Primula malacoides*.
- ❀ Sow cyclamen.
- ❀ Take softwood cuttings of pelargoniums, fuchsias, verbenas and penstemons.
- ❀ Start off freesias, lachenalias, arum lilies and nerines.
- ❀ Rest gloxinias.

VEGETABLES

- ❀ Sow lettuce for winter cropping.
- ❀ Harvest tomatoes, cucumbers, sweet peppers and aubergines.
- ❀ Train, feed and sideshoot tomatoes.
- ❀ Train and feed cucumbers.

FRUIT

- ❀ Water and feed vines carefully.
- ❀ Harvest peaches and nectarines.
- ❀ Harvest strawberries.
- ❀ Pot up newly rooted strawberry runners.

and the greenhouse is chock-a-block with plants threatening to get out of control. Colourful greenhouse climbers that are still giving their best include bougainvilleas, *Plumbago capensis*, lapagerias, passion flowers and *Cobaea scadens* (cathedral bell). Again the annual climbers like *Thunbergia alata*

KEEPING YOUR GREENHOUSE COOL

The temperature inside your greenhouse will soar as soon as the sun comes out. If the greenhouse is left closed with no protection, the temperature can reach well over 100°F (38°C) on a hot, summer's day. Most plants in a greenhouse stop growing if the temperature gets above 80°F (27°C) and will overheat if it gets much higher. Shade-loving plants such as ferns and ivies will show symptoms of heat stress at much lower temperatures. It is essential, therefore, to keep temperatures down, aiming to maximise plant growth and yields.

ORGANIZING YOUR GREENHOUSE

You can use the sun-loving plants in the greenhouse to provide some shade for the other plants. Tomatoes, for example, planted on the south-facing side can help shade the rest of the greenhouse from summer onwards. Staging, too, can be used to cast shadows for plants growing in the border early in the season. But however well you organize your greenhouse it won't stay cool unless you can let the heat escape.

VENTILATION

Opening vents to release the hot air from the greenhouse is the obvious answer. Maintaining an optimum growing temperature for your plants isn't easy, especially if you are out all day working. In early to mid-spring when early morning temperatures can be near zero and days calm and sunny, it is difficult to know whether to open the vents in the morning or take the chance of the greenhouse overheating during the day. Even in late spring the need for ventilation can change dramatically from hour to hour as heavy showers are interspersed by bright sunshine. The answer lies in automatic vents that respond to temperature fluctuations opening and, just as importantly, closing vents when necessary. There are a number of brands on the market for both hinged and louvred vents.

A greenhouse can be ventilated in two ways: either by making use of the fact that hot air rises (sometimes called the 'chimney' method); or by using air movement outside to cause air circulation inside the greenhouse ('breeze' method). The chimney method requires at least one vent in the roof and one near to ground level so that hot, moist air rising out of the roof vent is replaced by cooler, dryer air entering the side vent. The breeze method relies on the prevailing wind being diverted into the greenhouse by vents on the windward side, thereby pushing hot, moist air out of vents on the leeward side. Of course in calm conditions the breeze method is far less effective. Alternatively, you can install an electric fan to force air out on calm days.

It is essential to have sufficient ventilation for the size of you greenhouse. Ideally, aim for an open area of at least one-sixth of the floor area (*see* Greenhouse Equipment in Chapter 3). If your greenhouse does not have enough vents contact the manufacturer for a vent kit. They are easy to install, especially on an aluminium-framed greenhouse. Most manufacturers supply hinged roof and side vent kits as well as kits for louvred vents. Louvred vent kits cost about twice as much as hinged vent kits.

SHADING

Even with all the vents open, and the door too, you will not be able to keep a greenhouse cool enough in the height of summer if the weather is warm and sunny. To maintain the right growing temperature you will need to prevent some of the sun's energy entering the greenhouse by putting up temporary shading. Don't be in a hurry to cover the whole greenhouse however. There is rarely too much light for greenhouse plants so shading will inevitably cut down on growth and yields of greenhouse crops. It is a matter of timing to get the balance right. When you first notice that opening vents alone isn't sufficient to keep temperatures down, shade the sunny side of the greenhouse. When this is insufficient shading, shade the roof as well as the side that gets evening sun. Finally, if temperatures are still getting too high, shade the side that gets the morning sun. There is no need to shade the north-facing side of a greenhouse. As temperatures fall again in late summer, remove the shading from the sides that get morning and evening sun first, then remove it from the roof and finally from the south-facing side.

Putting up shading materials inside the greenhouse is less effective than washes applied to the glass or slatted blinds attached to the outside of the frame. This is because light energy from the sun turns to heat energy on contact with the shading, which if attached inside the greenhouse is trapped and contributes to the increasing air temperature. For most people the shading washes applied to the outside of the glass work out cheapest and easiest. There is even a product that turns transparent in the rain, so allowing more light in.

DAMPING DOWN

The other method of keeping a greenhouse cool and one advocated by professionals is regular damping down. This means wetting surfaces such as paths and staging. The water then absorbs energy as it evaporates and the hot moist air is allowed to escape through the vents, thereby cooling the greenhouse. To maximise this effect you need to dampen down regularly through the heat of the day which isn't practical for most people. Filling your greenhouse with plants and giving them plenty of water is easier and will have the same effect as plants will loose much of the water they absorb as water vapour on hot days.

(black-eyed Susan), which has orange plate-like flowers with purple eyes, and *Ipomoea* (morning glory) with its shining sky-blue trumpet blooms, are performing well and not showing any signs of slowing down.

Keeping the greenhouse cool enough is again the priority – see left. Use ventilation and shading to best effect to keep those desiccating sun rays at bay. Ventilate using both roof and side vents during the day, but still needing only roof vents at night. Watering must be given as often as required. This can mean two or three times a day for plants in small containers unless you have an automatic watering system. Plants in growing bags, like tomatoes and cucumbers, will be producing fruit all month and will require large amounts of water.

PROPAGATION

In early summer there is still time to sow *Primula malacoides* for a colourful display this winter – try varieties such as 'Bright Eyes Mixed' which has lovely combinations of carmine, rose, white, pink and purple. Further sowings of *P. kewensis* and *P. sinensis* can also be made. Scatter the seed thinly in a shallow seedtray filled with compost. Cover them very lightly and place the seedtray in a temperature of about 61°F (16°C) to achieve germination. Since the seed is so near the surface it is important to cover the seedtray with a sheet of glass or place it inside a polythene bag to prevent it from drying out. Lay a sheet of newspaper over the seedtray and keep it away from direct sunlight. Remove this paper as soon as the seed starts to germinate and place the seedtray in a lightly shaded position. When the seedlings are large enough to be handled they need to be pricked out singly into 3½in (9cm) pots filled with potting compost. Move them out to the cold frame to harden off.

Sow another batch of colourful cinerarias for autumn flowering. Sow thinly into a seedtray filled with seed compost and maintain a temperature of around 55°F (13°C). Prick out cinerarias sown last month when they are big enough to be handled safely. Don't prick out too many though – it is easy to get carried away!

Exacum.

HOLIDAYS

Holidays are another problem that face all but the most dedicated greenhouse gardeners during the summer months – who will only take them when the greenhouse is dormant. Late summer is the most popular time for taking holidays and yet there is a lot of work to be carried out in and around the greenhouse. What can be done?

Well, sympathetic neighbours are the obvious answer – greenhouse sitters who are willing and capable of holding the fort while you are away. But it's a lot to ask and how many of us have neighbours that can afford the time?

The only answer is to simplify matters. Reduce the management to checking a thermometer, switching on a button and turning on a tap. That's certainly straightforward enough, but how can we get all that needs to be done in the greenhouse down to just a few simple operations?

Automatic vents will be of great advantage and shading can already be in place, so that leaves watering. One option is to install a fully automatic watering system using reservoirs of water plumbed into the mains and water computers to control when plants are given water and how much is applied. If you decide to go down this route, make sure the system is fully operational a couple of weeks before you are due to go to iron out any teething problems.

Many plants can be removed from the scorching greenhouse and put into a sheltered spot in the garden. Make a plunge bed in a shady area. Water thoroughly before you leave and all will be well when you return. Plants that will not adjust to the climatic change must be kept in the greenhouse. Make a cheap, yet reliable, semi-automatic watering system using capillary matting.

Set the system up at least a week before the holiday to iron out last minute problems so that it's working like clockwork before you go. Do remember, though, that pots must not have crocks for drainage, nor rims on their bases because the capillary action cannot bridge these gaps and the pots will not receive any water.

Alpine species of calceolarias need to be sown this month as soon as the seeds are ripe. Prepare a seedtray of sowing compost and sow thinly by adding dry silver sand to the seed packet to act as a thinning agent. Place the seedtray in a greenhouse or cold frame where the seed will germinate. Pot-grown calceolarias for greenhouse display during the winter can still be sown this month if not already done.

Clearing out of the greenhouse of all potted up young plants destined for the garden can be completed this month. Stack empty pots and seedtrays ready for a cleaning binge later in the year. Remove the last of the temporary staging and give the rapidly growing greenhouse border plants, like tomatoes and cucumbers, all the space you can.

In mid-summer, try some winter-flowering pansies to brighten up the greenhouse display by sowing now outside in a prepared seedbed or in a cold frame. Germination will take only a couple of weeks and young seedlings will soon be ready to be pricked out. The variety 'Floral Dance Mixed', will, given reasonable weather, flower right through until the following spring. It is free-flowering with ruby, violet, white and yellow forms all available.

More cinerarias can be sown to continue the succession and those sown last month will be ready for pricking out into 3½in (9cm) pots using a potting compost. Even established seedlings will need plenty of shade now.

By mid-summer, alpine calceolarias will be producing ripe seed, so they need to be sown as soon as possible for best germination. Place the seedtray in a cool greenhouse or frame where the seeds will germinate. Seeds sown in early summer will need pricking out as soon as the seedlings are large enough to handle safely. Put them singly into 3½in (9cm) pots filled with potting compost and return them to the cold frame.

If you want a glorious show of heavily scented blooms in the greenhouse during the winter then make a sowing of stocks outside in a prepared seedbed this month. Choose a sheltered spot and keep well watered.

A winter display of mignonette, *Reseda odorata*, can be sown this month onwards. This valuable pot plant produces long, slender spikes densely packed with flowers that have a delicious morning and evening fragrance. Varieties like 'Fragrant Beauty' and 'Crimson Fragrance' tell their own story. Sow half a dozen seeds in a 5½in (14cm) pot, thinning them to leave the strongest three or four.

In late summer, many spring-flowering greenhouse pot plants can be sown. Sow thinly into a seedtray filled with sowing compost and keep at around 55°F (13°C) until germination has taken place. Cover with a sheet of glass and newspaper and place in a warm position. When the germinated seedlings are large enough to handle they should be pricked out into 3½in (9cm) pots filled with a potting compost. Place in a cold frame out of direct sunlight.

A final sowing of cinerarias can be made in late summer. For small greenhouses try the compact variety 'Gay Mixed' that produces an abundance of colourful blooms on a 10in (25cm) high plant. Also worth trying is 'Mini Scarlet Mixed' at only 8in (20cm) high and covered in 1½in (4cm) blooms.

Sow *Primula malacoides* if you want to produce whorls of stunning blooms on slender stems during early spring. Although most amateur seed catalogues no longer supply seed, the variety 'Bright Eyes Mixed' is still available and produces striking 8–10in (20–25cm) plants.

Hibiscus.

Also in late summer, the winter-flowering pansies can be sown in seedtrays or seedbeds outdoors or in a cold frame. The wide range of colours and delicate scent last well into spring. Sowings made last month should be pricked out as soon as they are large enough to handle safely.

If you want early spring-flowering clarkia in the greenhouse you'll need to sow the seed in a well-prepared seedbed this month or next. Pot up seedlings into 3½in (9cm) containers to grow on for a few weeks before moving them into their final 5½in (14cm) pots. Place in a cool greenhouse over winter so that they are ready for flowering in late winter or early spring.

Late-spring flowering nemesia can also be produced if seed is sown now. Aim to get 'three seedlings in a 6in (15cm) pot of potting compost by sowing five seeds and thinning out the weakest. Pinch out the remaining plants when they are well established to encourage bushy growth.

Schizanthus is another flowering pot plant recommended for small greenhouses. Try the well-loved 'Star Parade' or the newer F2 variety 'Disco', which makes a good garden plant, too. The compact orchid-like blooms produce outstanding displays for early summer. Sow thinly in a seedtray and cover lightly with compost this month. Kept at a temperature of around 50°F (10°C) they soon germinate. They can be potted up into 3½in (9cm) pots filled with potting compost as soon as they can be handled. Again, these benefit from being pinched out when they are well established to obtain thick bushy growth that support the weighty blooms in spring.

Cyclamen in shades from deep and rich purple to white flushed with pink bring warmth to the coldest rooms during the winter months. Late summer is the best time to sow cyclamen for flowering at Christmas the following year. Prick out sowings of pot-grown primulas and calceolarias for winter flowering. Place them individually into 3½in (9cm) pots filled with potting compost.

Many garden plants can be propagated by summer-struck cuttings (*see* box overleaf). The long warm days means they can root quickly ready for potting up in a matter of weeks. Much of the growth

CYCLAMEN

This is the last opportunity to sow the seed of large pot-grown cyclamen. They will be ready to flower at Christmas the following year. The alternative is to sow in mid- to late winter for small plants flowering at the end of the year. For best results:

1. Soak the seed for about twenty-four hours before sowing.

2. Then space the plump seed about 1in (2.5cm) apart in a pot filled with a half-and-half mix of sowing compost and grit.

3. Place the pot in a polythene bag in a warm 59°F (15°C), dark place.

4. At the first signs of germination, remove the bag and place the pot in a warm, light position out of direct sunlight.

5. Wait until the seedlings are touching before pricking out individually into 3½in (9cm) pots. At this stage, plant the tiny corms two-thirds proud of the compost surface and maintain a temperature of around 59°F 15°C. Water sparingly until new growth is apparent.

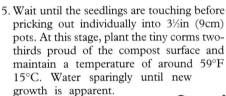

EARLY SUMMER CUTTINGS

Many herbaceous perennials like chrysanthemums, dahlias, lupins and delphiniums can be propagated now while the young shoots are soft. Select a healthy non-flowering shoot and cut it cleanly from the parent just above a leaf joint. Remove the lower leaves and trim to just below a leaf joint so that the cutting is about 4in (10cm) long. Stick the cutting in a gritty compost where it should root.

Many rock plants can also be propagated from cuttings, and if you want a lavender hedge take cuttings now. Select 3–4in (7.5–10cm) sideshoots during this month or next and remove the lower leaves and soft growing tips. Fill a 5½in (14cm) pot with a gritty compost and insert them in 1in (2.5cm) or so apart around the edge of the pot. Put a couple of short split canes in the pot, then place it in a clear plastic bag. Keep in the greenhouse out of direct sunlight and the cuttings will root within four or five weeks.

This is the time for taking leaf cuttings of streptocarpus and saintpaulias (*see* Chapter 5).

available, however, is soft and fleshy so it needs to be protected from the ravages of the sun and dry atmosphere.

The simplest solution is to stick cuttings directly into a closed atmosphere away from direct sunlight. The high humidity will prevent the cuttings wilting, so giving them time to root.

Flowering garden shrubs can be propagated by semi-ripe cuttings taken in mid-summer. Choose healthy semi-ripe shoots. That is, a shoot of current year's growth, soft at the tip but starting to ripen – producing a woody outer layer – at its base.

1. Select non-flowering shoots about 4in (10cm) long where possible and remove them from the parent plant with a heel of woody stem.

2. Trim the heel with a sharp knife so that there are no snags and remove lower leaves from the cutting. Dip the cut tip of each cutting in hormone rooting powder.

3. Fill a 5½in (14cm) pot with cuttings' compost or

make a well-drained rooting medium from peat and perlite, in a half-and-half mix. Water well.

4. Stick the cuttings around the edge of the pot using a narrow dibber or pencil to make the holes. Keep cuttings from wilting by placing in a mist unit or putting each pot into a clear plastic bag.

TIP

Where a garden frame is not available then a simple alternative can easily be made. A wooden box with a sheet of glass on top will do, or even a pot with a polythene bag top can be effective where only a few cuttings are planned. Once filled with cuttings, the box frame should be watered well, then closed and shaded. Keep an eye open for outbreaks of fungal diseases, spraying where necessary with systemic fungicide containing benomyl.

Hydrangea petiolaris can be increased by selecting healthy new growth and taking 3in (7.5cm) cuttings. Take off the lowest pair of leaves and trim the cuttings to just below the leaf joint. Remove the softest growing point to prevent wilting and stick in a well-drained gritty compost in a cold frame. When the cuttings are rooted pot them up.

Some cuttings are more difficult than others to root and so some form of bottom heat may be needed. Soil-warming cables in a frame or propagator on the greenhouse staging is the obvious remedy. Suitable subjects include abelia, forsythia, iberis, lithospermum, solanum, pittesporum, potentilla, pyracantha, philadelphus, escallonia, kolkwitzia, lonicera, cotoneaster, caryopteris and weigela.

Tender plants such as fuchsias, verbenas and penstemons can be propagated from healthy non-flowering shoots. Take a 3–4in (7.5–10cm) cutting and trim just below a leaf joint, remove lower leaves and dip base in a hormone rooting powder. Insert around the edge of a 3½in (9cm) pot filled with a gritty compost, then water and place in a closed frame or seal in a plastic bag. For best results maintain a temperature around 65°F (18°C). By mid-autumn the cuttings will have rooted and can be potted on individually into 3½in (9cm) pots.

Late summer is the best time for taking cuttings from many showy greenhouse plants including abutilon, *Cissis antartica* (kangaroo vine), citrus, croton,

---

TAKING PELARGONIUM CUTTINGS STEP-BY-STEP

Propagate pelargoniums in late summer from softwood cuttings. Both the zonal and ivy-leaf bedding types are easy to increase in number by selecting healthy, non-flowering shoots about 5in (12.5cm) long.

1. Using a sharp knife, cut them cleanly from the parent plant without leaving a snag.

2. Trim each shoot to just below a leaf joint to produce a 3in (7.5cm) cutting, then remove the lower leaves. Dipping in hormone powder is not normally necessary.

Trimmed cutting

3. Insert prepared cuttings either around the edge of a 6in (15cm) pot or individually into a 2½in (6cm) pots containing a sandy compost. Do not let the cuttings wilt before putting them in the pot and keep out of direct sunlight afterwards.

4. Water well and place in a sheltered spot.

datura, hibiscus, *Passiflora* (passion flower), philo-
dendron and verbena.

Select young, firm, healthy shoots about 4in
(10cm) long and trim below a leaf joint, using a
sharp knife. Trim off lower leaves and dip cut end
in hormone rooting powder. Insert around the edge
of a 3½in (9cm) pot filled with gritty compost and
place in a closed frame or seal in a polythene bag.

Passiflora violacea *'Empress'*.

Many more garden plants will be producing
suitable material for semi-ripe cuttings in late summer including ceratostigma, fatshederas, hebe,
hypericum, jasmine, sambucus and viburnum. If
you did not take cuttings of escallonia, philadelphus and weigela in mid-summer, it is not too late
to do so now.

PLANTING OUT

In early summer, the last of the chrysanthemum
cuttings taken in early spring will be ready to hard-
en off before being planted out into the garden.
Greenhouse azaleas can be placed in a shady sheltered spot outside in mid-summer for their summer
holiday. This helps ripen the shoots to promote
flowering next year. Plunge the pots into soil so they
don't dry out too quickly and water as necessary.

Cuttings taken in mid-summer will soon be showing signs of rooting by becoming fully turgid and
even putting on fresh growth. They must now be
removed from the plastic bag or propagator and
weaned off to the less humid greenhouse atmosphere. After a week or so they'll need potting on individually into 3½in (9cm) pots using a potting compost. They are best kept in a cold frame over winter
rather than being planted out in the garden borders.

DIVIDING CYCLAMEN

Check resting tubers because they'll soon be
shooting away. Where tubers are getting too big
for their pot they can either be potted on into a
larger container using a fresh compost or divided.

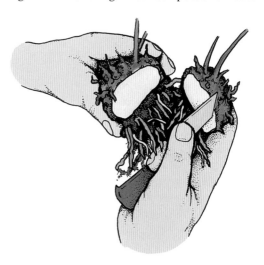

Divide them as soon as the buds start to show by
cutting the tubers into two or three pieces, using a
sharp knife. Make sure each section of the tuber
has a healthy, plump bud. To protect against fungal infections it's a good idea to dip the cut surface
in a fungicidal powder such as 'flowers of sulphur'.
Pot up the tuber sections in a potting compost so
that the crown is standing proud of the surface.
Water well and place in a cool, shaded position.

Vegetables and Fruit

In early summer, strawberry plants for next year
should be selected from runners being produced on
garden plants. Several varieties are suitable for
forcing including 'Gorella', 'Pantagruella', 'Red

Peg out strawberry runners into 3½in (9cm) pots filled with compost.

Sow seed individually 2in (5cm) apart each way in a standard seedtray or in modular seedtrays filled with sowing compost. Plant out 8–10in (20–25cm) apart in early mid-autumn as soon as seedlings are large enough to handle. Where a minimum temperature of around 45°F (7°C) can be maintained, varieties like 'Colombus', 'Kellys', 'Kloek' and 'Ravel' can be sown to produce a succession of crisp heads all winter long. Sow late autumn onwards.

POTTING ON AND PLANTING

Rooted cuttings of pelargoniums and fuchsias that have outgrown their 3½in (9cm) pots should be potted on into 5in (12.5cm) containers using a potting compost. Similarly, pot on any perpetual-flowering carnations if you have not already done so.

Christmas-flowering freesias can be obtained if you start plump, healthy corms in late summer. Their delicately branching sprays make ideal cut flowers for the festive season and fill the house with a lovely scent. Place about six or eight in a 6in (15cm) pot of potting compost so that they are about 1in deep. Water and place in a cool greenhouse or frame or in a sheltered spot outside. Keep watering sparingly until the first growths are apparent. Those pots started outside must be brought indoors before the first cold snap of early autumn.

Elegant lachenalias, better known as the Cape cowslip should be potted up late summer as well. In pots or hanging baskets their striking colourful bell-like blooms make a superb display. Again, place six bulbs in a 6in (15cm) pot filled with potting compost, then cover with a further inch or so, Water well. Don't water again until growth is visible. Keep in a cool ventilated greenhouse or frame. Alternatively make use of your spring hanging baskets by cleaning them out and filling them with lachenalias.

Gauntlet', 'Cambridge Vigour' and 'Rival'. Choose strong healthy runners and peg them down into a 3½in (9cm) pots, buried nearly up to their rim in the soil and filled with compost.

Towards late summer, sow a tray of lettuce such as 'Cynthia', 'Novita' or 'Kwiek', for planting into the greenhouse border when it becomes vacant.

HARDENING OFF

In early summer, move out vegetables such as aubergines, capsicums, marrows and ridge cucumbers sown in mid-spring to be hardened off, if not already done. These can then be planted out as soon as space becomes available.

POLLINATION

As new trusses develop on tomato plants and the flowers open you can systematically go round the greenhouse and lightly tap each truss to distribute pollen, although this isn't always necessary. Some growers like to damp down the crop in order to help pollination. Whatever the method, it is best done just before the warmest part of the day.

Lachenalia.

The much underrated nerine (the Guernsey lily) is another bulb ready to be started into growth after the summer's rest. *N. bowdeni* produces up to ten rich pink large florets that make excellent cut flowers. Pot up one, two or three bulbs into 3½, 4 or 6in (9, 10 or 15cm) pots respectively so that the neck of the bulb is visible. Place in a cold frame, water sparingly until the first foliage appears. Bring into the heated greenhouse or living room to flower. Take care not to overfeed, otherwise they'll produce a lot of leaves at the expense of blooms.

New strawberry runners selected in early summer pinned down in to 3in (7.5cm) pots filled with compost should now have rooted sufficiently to be liberated from their parent plants. Water and feed as necessary to produce strong healthy stock for next year. Later in the month they'll probably be ready for potting on into 6in (15cm) containers filled with a peat-based potting compost.

Place the plant to one side of the pot, with the growing point facing outwards. This will be helpful next year when the plants are fruiting since they will then dangle over the edge of the pot and not in the compost where they can become wet and rot.

TRAINING, PRUNING AND THINNING

Flowers

Chrysanthemums grown for a garden display of flowers should have their growing tips pinched out, when shoots from the first stopping are at least 12in (30cm) long. This will encourage many flowering stems, producing a multitude of smaller blooms.

Stop chrysanthemums to encourage flowering stems.

Spray varieties will need pinching out again before the onset of mid-summer. Greenhouse chrysanthemums should be stopped for the first time about a month later, with spray varieties' second pinching carried out in mid-summer.

As soon as perpetual-flowering carnations have produced about eight pairs of leaves, pinch them back to five. When sideshoots are produced from the leaf joints, they too will need to be stopped so that the plants will break again.

If you leave some sideshoots to flower they will bloom earlier than those left alone. Using this method you can achieve an almost continuous show of blooms throughout the winter months.

Disbud dahlias: either pinch out the main bud and allow the two sidebuds to develop, or pinch out the sidebuds (as shown here), leaving the main bud to flower.

DISBUDDING

Early chrysanthemums should be disbudded in mid-summer: remove all the buds and sideshoots that develop from leaf joints down the stem, so that only the terminal bud remains. Spray varieties are not disbudded.

Vegetables and Fruit

Continue to train the early sowings of tomato plants by either adding new ties where raffia ties are being used or winding the string around new growth where the string method is being employed.

Removing sideshoots from tomatoes must be carried out as a matter of routine – at least once and preferably twice a week this month. Remove small sideshoots by holding the plant beneath a leaf joint with one hand and bending the sideshoot over at 90 degrees, first one way and then the other. The sideshoot will snap out cleanly.

Larger shoots missed on previous occasions should be cut out using a sharp pruning knife. If there is any disease in the greenhouse then dip your knife in a fungicidal solution like 'Bordeaux Mixture' between cuts.

The most important shoots to remove are those directly below a flower truss since they are often the most vigorous and if left to grow will take sap flow away from the truss, reducing its yield. Check for pests and diseases while removing sideshoots.

Late in the season, stop tomatoes as they reach 6in (15cm) above the top supporting wire to encourage the quick development of fruit so they have all ripened by the autumn – it takes about eight weeks for tomatoes to develop and ripen at this time of year. However, if you want tomatoes after this period then let the plants grow up to the eaves.

Lower leaves will start to yellow and should be removed. In fact, at this stage it's worth removing leaves up to the first truss to let air circulate around the fruit. Some people also thin leaves – that is, remove one of the three leaves that develop between trusses.

WHITEFLY

Whitefly can be a real problem in the greenhouse because they are difficult to control at egg and larval stages. To overcome their resistance to chemical control it is necessary to make repeat treatments every four to seven days for about three weeks. In this way all the whitefly in the greenhouse will have been treated at adult stage at least once.

Training cucumber plants up secure wires must continue during the early summer. Tie the stem loosely, but securely, to the wire using loops of string. Stop the cucumber plants by pinching out the growing tip when they reach the roof.

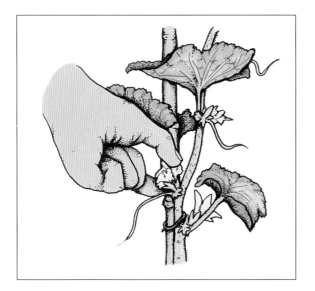

Remove male flowers from cucumber plants.

Systematically stop all lateral shoots back to the second leaf joint and, if you are not growing the all-female variety, pinch out all male flowers (those without the swelling behind the flower). Remove female flowers from the main stem on all varieties.

Aubergines and sweet peppers under glass need staking in early summer if this has not already been done. Place a cane about an inch (2.5cm) from the main stem.

The laterals of melons planted in frames will need to be stopped as they reach the corners of the frame. Subsequent sub-laterals will produce male and female flowers that will need pollinating. (*see* Spring, Chapter 6).

Late in the summer, melons will need supporting with a net as they swell. This should be securely attached to an overhead supporting wire. Melons are ripe when the surface around the stem begins to crack.

GRAPES

Grapes should be thinned out in early summer, and this should be done in two stages. First make sure you have a suitable pair of scissors and a supporting stick with a forked tip to hold bunches apart while they are thinned (*see also* Spring) – do not touch the fruit with your hands because if the bloom is spoilt it reduces the fruit's natural defences.

Check the centre of the bunch and remove most of the grapes. This allows air circulation through the bunch. Then remove small and imperfect berries. Finally, the bunch should be thinned to give each berry remaining enough room to swell to full size.

The top or shoulder of the bunch will need less thinning than the centre if you are to preserve the classical shape of a bunch of grapes. Tie the shoulder of the bunch to a supporting wire using several loops of string.

Late-started vines will need their first thinning in mid-summer and, as with the earlier vines, will often need a second thinning about a month after the first. This involves checking the bunch over and removing any small or malformed berries. Then check through the bunch to ensure that there is enough room for their final weeks of development and growth. Check that the string tying each bunch to the supporting wire isn't constricting, and add any extra ties where necessary.

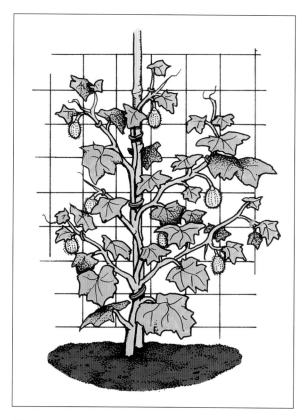

Tie melons securely to a large-mesh support.

FEEDING, WATERING, HEAT AND SHADE

Flowers

Where chrysanthemums are being grown for their large blooms they will need careful watering and feeding from early summer. Perpetual-flowering carnations will need adequate shading during the

---

RESTING

Early-started gloxinias will be showing signs of yellowing by late summer. Reduce watering slowly to nothing, removing dead flowers and leaves regularly to prevent diseases getting a hold in the resting tuber. Store in a warm 54°F (12°C) dry place out of direct sunlight. Be decisive when throwing out tubers – keep only young healthy stock.

---

hottest weather and a stake in each pot will provide support. do not feed perpetual flowering carnations until the flowerbuds show, but keep well watered and damp down the greenhouse floor on scorching days.

Vegetables

When aubergine and sweet pepper flowers open, spray to help fruit set. Water as necessary and feed every fortnight with a liquid fertilizer. Both these crops are compatible with cucumbers so they can all be grown together at one end of the greenhouse. Watch out for greenfly and whitefly, spraying where necessary.

Feed all tomato plants using a high potash tomato fertilizer. Sowings made at the beginning of the year will be carrying rapidly swelling and ripening fruit by early summer. Watering is of critical importance now – applications every day may be necessary if the weather is warm. Ventilation is important, too, so open vents and even the door on hot sunny days, and top vents on still, mild evenings.

Growing bags containing greedy crops like tomatoes, cucumbers and melons will need regular feeding at least once a week during early summer. Liquid feeds are far better than powder because they are instantly available to the plant. With such large amounts of feed being applied to so little compost there is going to be a risk of salt building up and

It is very important to feed and water tomatoes regularly throughout the growing season.

damaging roots. To avoid this ensure that the bag is watered heavily with pure water to wash the excess salts away.

Continue to feed, sideshoot and remove yellowing leaves throughout the summer, and water as required.

It takes about eight weeks for fruit to develop, swell and ripen. So where tomatoes are being grown in an unheated greenhouse it would be a good idea to pinch out the growing tip to encourage those fruits already set to develop at full speed.

Cucumbers will need shading if not already provided, so apply a proprietary whitewash or hang one of the various netting materials available. Damp down the greenhouse and plants each day to keep up the healthy humidity but restrict watering to just a couple of times a week. Those grown in mounds on border soil will require top dressing with compost when roots start to show through the surface.

Ventilate on hot days, not letting the temperature rise above 90°F (32°C) and aiming for about 77°F (25°C). Don't lose all the humidity otherwise there will be outbreaks of damaging spider mite.

In late summer, feed and water as necessary. Make sure the temperature doesn't get too high nor the humidity too low. Check whitewash shading to make sure it hasn't been washed off by summer rain.

HOT SUMMERS

In very warm years actively growing tomatoes, cucumbers and melon plants in the greenhouse may well need watering more than once a day if you are to achieve the maximum yield possible. If this is not practical – if you are out at work for instance – then it's worth investing in some form of continuous trickle irrigation. If you are growing in bags, then automatic irrigation is a great help in average summers, too.

In early summer, peaches and nectarines should be checked regularly to make sure they have enough water while the fruits are swelling. Start feeding and carry it right through until the end of summer.

Those with ripening fruit should not be sprayed, but ventilate both top and bottom, providing the temperatures don't fall too low. Keep a special look out for spider mite while damping down has been abandoned since this pest thrives in a drier atmosphere.

In late summer, those plants that have already been harvested can be sprayed daily again to increase humidity and to keep spider mite and thrips at bay. Ventilate both top and bottom.

MELONS

Reduce the humidity for the melons as the early fruits start to swell. Don't let the daytime temperature fall too low, though. Remember to water and feed with care as necessary and keep an eye open for pests and diseases.

Later in the summer, place pieces of wood or tiles under rapidly swelling melons in garden frames to protect them from the soil.

Water and feed strawberries as the fruits swell. If there has been a very good set it might well be worth thinning them to improve their size. All misshapen, badly set fruit should be removed and discarded. Keep the greenhouse well ventilated on warm, sunny days, but don't let the temperature drop too low. Keep an eye open for pests and diseases. In late summer especially, check fruit daily for outbreaks of grey mould, picking off any affected fruit. Water carefully as necessary.

Harvest strawberries as soon as they are ripe.

WATERING

Keeping container plants and to a lesser extent plants grown in the greenhouse border well watered is perhaps the most important task for the greenhouse gardener. In the height of summer a couple of growing bags filled with tomatoes may need as much as a watering can full of water a day. Since you can only apply a few pints to each at any one time that means watering at least twice and sometimes three times a day. Plants in smaller containers such as pot plants on staging, say, or young plants in small pots, will need watering even more often. If you are not able to water during the day you can either accept poor growth and lower yields that result from the plants' discomfort at going short of water, or you will need to rig up some form of automatic watering system.

CAPILLARY MATTING SYSTEM

For pot plants, capillary matting is the simplest and cheapest solution. This system comprises a thick felty matting laid on a flat, waterproof surface. The matting absorbs water and will pass on that water to any pots and containers stood upon it via capillary action. Containers must have flat bottoms and there must not be any crocks in their base otherwise the compost in the pot cannot absorb the water. Pots larger than 6in (15cm) deep will not draw up sufficient water from capillary action and so will need watering from the top too. Water will evaporate from the mat, so keeping the matting wet will need regular watering. To reduce evaporation you can cover the matting in black polythene with holes cut for the base of each pot. To keep the matting constantly wet it's worth making it semi-automatic by trailing an end into a reservoir such as a plastic trough. The trough can then be filled periodically as required. This system can be made fully automatic by

plumbing it into the mains and having the reservoir topped up through a ball-cock valve (rather like those used for toilet cisterns).

DRIP AND TRICKLE SYSTEM

A second option that's suitable for larger pots, growing bags and plants grown in borders, is a drip and trickle system. This is basically a series of fine tubes that direct water from the mains via a hosepipe or from a reservoir by gravity to individual pots or plants. At the end of each tube is a nozzle that allows water to drip or trickle out at a very slow rate. This rate can be adjusted to suit the needs of each individual plant. The mains supply can be fitted with a water timer or computer so that you can control when watering takes place.

SEEP HOSE SYSTEM

This is simply a perforated hosepipe that allows water to trickle out along its length. It could be used in the greenhouse for border crops and growing bags but isn't as accurate as a drip system. However, it's a lot cheaper to install and takes little or no maintenance.

TIMERS AND WATER COMPUTERS

There are two types of water computer; timers that allow water to flow for a set period and then turn off the supply; and programmers that will turn the water on and off at the times set.

The simplest and cheapest system is the timer. There are models that will allow water to flow for a given time or allow a set number of gallons through before switching off the supply. There's nothing much to choose between them, so which one you buy really depends on personal preference.

Watering computers are as easy to programme as central heating controls. They will turn the water supply on and off when you want and operate up to six separate watering systems in a garden. For the greenhouse gardener this offers great control over watering during the day and can be programmed to continue watering while you're away on holiday.

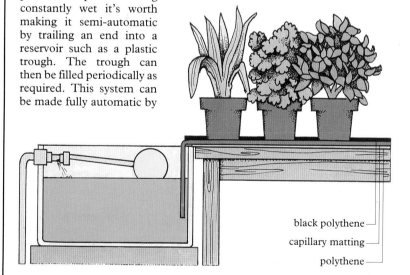

black polythene
capillary matting
polythene

As the first fruits start to colour up it is important to keep the atmosphere dry so ventilate freely. Stop feeding at this point, but continue to water as necessary, taking great care not to splash the berries since this encourages botrytis or grey mould. If an outbreak of botrytis does occur, then remove the affected fruit and spray the rest with a fungicide containing benomyl. Keep an eye open for greenfly that will plague strawberry plants given half a chance.

To get good quality fruit from your grape vines careful watering and feeding must be a priority throughout the growing and, in particular, the fruiting season. Water thoroughly once a week or so, increasing the amounts given in response to hot weather. Give gallons of water each time to get moisture deep into the soil. Don't water little and often.

Feed the vine thoroughly in the growing season with a fertilizer high in potash. Tomato fertilizer is ideal, given every other week while the vine is growing, starting just around flowering time.

Ties holding bunches of grapes should also be checked to ensure they are not constricting sap flow and are providing ample support.

HARVESTING

Harvest as soon as cucumbers have reached a suitable size. Never leave fruit on a plant to get old since this stops the younger ones from developing.

Once laterals have finished fruiting they should be removed and a new one trained in its place to extend the cropping season. In late summer, frame-grown cucumbers will have matured, so if you have a crop then remove the ageing plants from your greenhouse. If not, keep greenhouse cucumbers cropping by cutting out old laterals and training new ones. Remove plants that have finished cropping.

Tomatoes will be ready for harvesting throughout the summer. Keep a careful eye on watering to ensure you don't get problems like fruit splitting and blossom end rot that are associated with erratic watering.

Sweet peppers can be harvested when they start to sound hollow when tapped. If red fruits are wanted pick them when they are just starting to turn, then ripen them fully in the kitchen. You can, if you prefer, let them ripen to red on the plant but

Sweetpeppers can be harvested when they feel hollow when tapped. It is best to harvest them green and allow them to ripen in the kitchen.

this will reduce subsequent fruit production considerably because the plant slows right down.

Aubergines, too, will be ripening for harvest in late summer. Pick them as soon as they are ripe and don't be tempted to harvest more than eight fruits off one plant because size and time will be lost.

Harvest peaches and nectarines as soon as they are ripe – they turn a yellowish hue and give slightly when pressed lightly in the palm.

With melons, the skin around the stem on the melon starts to crack when they are ripe. You'll be in no doubt when they are ripe because they fill the greenhouse with a sweet aroma.

Harvest strawberries as they ripen and keep the atmosphere dry through good ventilation.

Once plants have finished fruiting they are of no further value, so should be consigned to the compost heap.

Harvest all fruit as they become ripe. If you are lucky enough to have a glut of fruit, excess can be stored perfectly well in a cool place.

CHAPTER 8

Autumn

GENERAL MANAGEMENT

Early Autumn

As the summer nears its end, the nights become distinctly colder and the days shorter. With the onset of autumn comes the end of many summer-flowering greenhouse plants. Beautiful greenhouse climbers such as bougainvilleas, *Corbaea scandens*, passiflora, thunbergia and ipomoea all continue to bloom, but the display slowly tails off.

Pelargoniums and fuchsias are an inspiration to us all as they soldier on producing bloom after bloom. It's little wonder they are among Britain's favourites when they are such good value for money.

The petunias and streptocarpus are also still blooming, but, again, their best days are now over.

Heating may be necessary during a cold snap and so all heating equipment must be overhauled by the

Regal pelargonium.

EARLY AUTUMN QUICK-REFERENCE CHECKLIST

❀ Overhaul heating equipment.
❀ Ventilate and water carefully, as this is important.
❀ Remove permanent shading.

FLOWERS

❀ Sow hardy annuals.
❀ Sow cyclamen.
❀ Start cyclamen corms and arum lilies.
❀ Start freesias and lilies in pots.
❀ Pot up prepared bulbs for forcing.
❀ Check cuttings.
❀ Take cuttings of evergreens and bedding plants.

VEGETABLES

❀ Harvest tomatoes, cucumbers, sweet peppers and aubergines.
❀ Harvest melons when ripe.
❀ Prick out lettuce.

FRUIT

❀ Check temperature changes in greenhouses containing ripening grapes.
❀ Check for pests and disease.
❀ Harvest peaches and nectarines.

end of the summer. Check also that flues are clear and fuel supplies are readily available.

Ventilation will be used less frequently depending on the weather conditions. In a warm spell both roof and side vents will be needed, but on cooler days ridge vents only will be necessary. Aim for day temperatures of about 59°F (15°C). At night the temperature will be dropping quite low so ventilate sparingly so that the greenhouse maintains a minimum of around 46°F (8°C). Damp down in the morning during warm spells and let the greenhouse slowly dry out towards evening. Don't forget to close the vents a couple of hours before the sun goes down to capture the last of the day's heat.

Check the vents have not been distorted during the summer so that they sit snugly on their frame without gaping cracks. It is essential to seal leaky vents if you are to maintain a minimum night temperature without resorting to expensive heating.

Less and less shading will be required as autumn progresses. Remove the permanent shading first so that the remaining temporary material can be removed and replaced according to the weather. Proprietary whitewash material can be removed with warm water and a scrubbing brush. It is important to remove all traces because light levels in the greenhouse during the winter can be critical. Maintain a permanent shade only over established shade-lovers.

Reduce watering as temperatures drop and growth rates slow down. Take care not to over-water. Use an insecticide smoke to control late infestations of whitefly, spider mite and aphids.

Plants that have stood outside during the summer will soon need to return to the greenhouse. Watch the weather forecast for cold snaps – particularly if it is windy – and move tender plants inside. Check them over carefully so that no pests or diseases are introduced unwittingly into the greenhouse.

Mid-autumn

Chrysanthemums in the greenhouse really come into their own now. Decorative varieties with large, intricate blooms in a kaleidoscope of colours stand tall on 3ft (1m) stems. A fair amount of space is necessary, but the effect is quite spectacular when the crop is in full glory. Perpetual-flowering carnations complement the chrysanthemums; although not nearly so showy, their blooms have unmistakable appeal.

This is usually the wettest period of the year. It is a good time to start bringing in the remaining tender plants after their summer holiday in the garden since stormy and colder weather soon prevails.

Nights will be drawing in quickly and days shortening to provide precious little time for evening gardening. Temperatures will drop considerably with an increased threat of frost at night. Aim to keep the greenhouse temperature above 45°F (7°C) by the judicious use of heating and ventilation. Daytime temperatures around 54°F (12°C) are easier to maintain, but some heat will inevitably be needed on cold, damp days when the weather closes in. It's worth considering whether you close down part of your greenhouse for the colder winter months to save on

---

MID-AUTUMN QUICK-REFERENCE CHECKLIST

Dahlia 'Collarette Dandy'.

❀ Check heating equipment and thermostats.
❀ Cut down on ventilation.
❀ Water sparingly.
❀ Close down part of the greenhouse if not fully utilized.

FLOWERS

❀ Sow sweet peas for the show bench.
❀ Prick out seedlings.
❀ Rest tuberous begonias and gloxinias.
❀ Last chance to start freesias.
❀ Pot up spring-flowering bulbs.
❀ Take conifer cuttings.
❀ Label dahlias in the garden.

VEGETABLES

❀ Harvest tomatoes and sweet peppers.
❀ Sow lettuce in greenhouse for succession.

FRUIT

❀ Harvest grapes.
❀ Ripen new wood on peaches and nectarines.
❀ Water strawberries carefully.

heating bills. Partition off a section with a roof vent and a heat supply using polythene, or preferably bubble matting to give a good insulation layer.

Ventilation will be restricted to daytime only. On still, bright days open the vents a couple of hours after dawn and close them again a couple of hours before dusk. This will trap as much heat energy as possible from the sun and keep heating bills to a minimum. Ventilate more freely if the temperature rises above 68°F (20°C), but use roof vents only – side vents will cause damaging draughts of cold air to sweep through the soft greenhouse plants. Greenhouses heated by non-flue gas or paraffin heaters will need to be ventilated to prevent the build-up of noxious fumes given off as a by-product of combustion. Water vapour, too, is produced and so this must be ventilated out to reduce the risk of diseases. Cold greenhouses containing hardy plants should be ventilated during the winter to lower the incidence of moulds and mildews.

If you are intending to buy a greenhouse heater, buy during autumn before many tender favourites are lost to the winter weather. An electric heater such as a portable fan heater is useful to start with because it is simple to use, takes very little space and requires next to no maintenance. It also has the added advantage of being able to circulate the air, which helps to reduce the incidence of fungal attacks. It also distributes heat in the greenhouse keeping all plants safe. Where only a few plants need to be kept from the icy clutches then it may well be more economical to invest in a heated propagating frame or propagator rather than a heater. Water sparingly all this month, taking care not to splash sensitive plants like primulas and cyclamen.

Also check around the garden for any forgotten tender perennials or half-hardy plants that need to be protected in the greenhouse to survive the winter. Check over the plants to remove yellowing leaves and overwintering pests.

Late Autumn

The weather at this time of the year is dominated by one system of rain-bearing clouds after another.

Chrysanthemums in the greenhouse – protected from these damaging storms – still dominate the floral display with their fabulous decorative blooms

---

LATE AUTUMN QUICK-REFERENCE CHECKLIST

❀ Restrict ventilation and give careful watering.
❀ Check heaters regularly.
❀ Annual greenhouse clean-up campaign.

FLOWERS

❀ Label Chrysanthemums.
❀ Pot up *Iris reticulata* and *Helleborous niger*.

VEGETABLES

❀ Blanch chicory and seakale.
❀ Lift rhubarb crowns for forcing.
❀ Sow lettuce for continuity of supply.

FRUIT

❀ Prune vines once dormant.
❀ Ventilate peaches, nectarines and strawberries.

---

in a wide range of colours. The white and yellow forms are particularly useful as cut flowers because they brighten up the short, dull days of autumn. Perpetual-flowering carnations also have their place with their continual production of double blooms in a variety of shades.

Cold, damp days and long nights means that cautious watering and ventilation are essential. Keep ventilators closed at night, only opening roof vents during warm, sunny days when there is little wind. Again, restrict ventilation to the period around midday making sure that they are shut down a couple of hours before dusk to trap as much of the sun's free energy as possible.

More heat will be needed as autumn progresses. For the majority of over-wintered greenhouse plants, maintain a night temperature of around 45°F (7°C) and a daytime one of about 54°F (12°C), on those rare sunny days ventilate above 68°F (20°C).

Automatic vents can be a problem when you want to close down the greenhouse a couple of hours before dusk so this is a good time to disconnect and service them. Automatic watering should also be disconnected if not already done and then cleaned and packed away for the winter. Any remaining shading should be removed and glass cleaned thoroughly to allow all available light to penetrate the greenhouse.

AUTUMN CLEAN-UP

1. Empty greenhouse, remove debris and dig over borders.

2. Scrub wooden structures and staging with garden disinfectant.

3. Wash glass thoroughly using garden disinfectant.

4. Clean out algae and dirt that will have accumulated in the glass overlaps. A plant label is ideal for this job.

5. Scrub aluminium mouldings with an old toothbrush.

6. Remove any shading paint from the glass with water and scrubbing brush.

It is important to give your greenhouse a thorough clean once a year and the quiet days of autumn provide the ideal opportunity. Pack up all the empty pots and seedtrays and move them out of the greenhouse. Choose a mild, sunny day when there is little or no wind. Take plants out of the greenhouse one by one, cleaning them up as you go and removing any dead and dying leaves. Prune if necessary. Place each pot in a sheltered spot. If the plants are particularly precious or particularly vulnerable take them indoors.

Once all the plants you wish to keep have been removed safely, it's time to start on the rubbish. Clear everything out, piling bits into plastic sacks or a wheelbarrow, and dump it on the compost heap, having first removed dead plants, old growing bags and any other debris. Separate any non-compostable stuff out and consign it to the dustbin. Then go around the empty greenhouse and pick off any bits of string from overhead wires, before scrubbing the entire structure with a stiff brush. Scrub down staging and shelving with a diluted horticultural disinfectant. Make certain all joints are cleaned out. Wash down the glass inside and out to remove algae and other dirt to allow maximum light penetration. Pay particular attention to the grime that accumulates in glass overlaps.

Replace rotten timbers in wooden-framed greenhouses – usually associated with algae growth around joints. Clear out gutters and wash seedtrays and pots. Aluminium frames should be rubbed down with wire wool or a stiff brush to dislodge dirt from aluminium sections.

Choose one of the water-based, plant-safe preservatives to treat the wood staging in the greenhouse structure, including any shelving. A couple of coats may be necessary if it has been neglected for a long time. Replace sagging wire and cracked panes of glass. Then clean out the runners of sliding doors and oil the bearings and hinges. Dig over the border soil and remove any missed debris, then water with a soil sterilant.

While the greenhouse is empty it's an ideal opportunity to put up insulation without all the usual fuss (*see* Winter, Chapter 9). Finally, return plants when it is safe to do so.

PROPAGATION

Flowers

Pots of heavily scented flowers in rich colours look stunning during dull winter days. Make sowings of half-hardy annuals such as stocks, schizanthus, clarkia, godetia, calendula, larkspur, anchusa,

---

CUTTINGS

Check cuttings to make sure they aren't wilting or succumbing to rot. Once rooted they should be potted up individually in 3½in (9cm) pots and placed in a cold frame or a cold greenhouse to overwinter.

Many evergreens can be propagated from semi-ripe cuttings this month. Select sideshoots of the current year's growth with firm bases showing slightly woody coloration. Sideshoots between 3–5in (7.5–12.5cm) long are best – any longer and there is a tendency to dry out without rooting. The material should be of healthy growth and be free of all pests and diseases. Each sideshoot should be ripening well at the base where it joins the parent and when pulled off should come away with a short 'heel' of bark (*see also* Propagation, Chapter 5). Suitable subjects include × *Cupressocyparis leylandii*, all types of *chamaecyparis, thuja, taxas, picea, juniperus* as well as *Cryptomeria japonica*.

You can continue taking cuttings of conifers until the end of mid-autumn and get well-rooted plants by late spring. This is not the quickest method of propagation, but it is simple and requires little aftercare.

Transfer pots of cuttings to a closed propagation case or cold frame where they will be able to root before drying out. Alternatively, place two short canes in the pot and place the whole thing in a polythene bag. The stakes will support the bag and prevent it touching the cuttings, which can cause rotting.

Water sparingly from now on and keep cuttings fairly dry during the winter months.

Try growing cuttings with a little bottom heat if you want them to root before winter. This can be achieved by soil-warming cables or a heated propagator. Remember, though, that although these cuttings are perfectly hardy, and indeed need a winter rest period if they have been given bottom heat, they should be weaned off the heat slowly.

❀ It's worth noting that to maintain the prostrate habit of ground-hugging conifers it is necessary to select material from the sides and not sideshoots pointing skywards.

nemophila, and salpiglossis. Sow in a well-prepared seedbed now, if not already done. If sown last month, seedlings will soon be ready to be potted up into 3½in (9cm) containers and placed in a cool greenhouse to get established.

Sweetpeas sown in mid-autumn will be well established early in the season, allowing them to produce larger and longer displays than those sown in spring. This is the best time to sow if the blooms are destined for the show bench.

Vegetables

Greenhouses heated to around 50°F (10°C) through the winter can support a crop of tender French beans. Sow 2in (5cm) deep in a large pot – 10in (25cm) – filled with a peat-based potting compost. If you have room, try a climbing variety, otherwise opt for a dwarf variety, such as 'Masterpiece' that can be grown in pots or the greenhouse border.

Prick out lettuce seedlings when they are large enough to handle safely, and make further sowings for continuity of supply. In mid-autumn, space seed 2in (5cm) apart each way in a standard seedtray, or individually into a modular seedtray filled with a peat-based sowing compost. Plant out 8–10in (20–25cm) apart in the greenhouse border before the seedlings start to touch in the seedtray.

In heated greenhouses (minimum 45°F; 7°C) sow varieties like 'Klock' and 'Revel' for maturing in early spring. There is also still time to sow a variety such as 'Kwiek' in a cold greenhouse to mature from mid-spring onwards. Continue lettuce through the winter by sowing further batches of 'Colombus' and 'Kellys'.

This is also the time to sow broad beans.

PLANTING AND FORCING

Many greenhouse flowers that have enjoyed a summer's rest can be started into growth this month to fill the greenhouse with colour and fragrance, from Christmas onwards. Mature cyclamen, for instance should be cleaned of any dead, dry foliage. Repot into the old container using fresh compost. Water sparingly at first to encourage them to start into growth.

Arum lilies are ready for starting in early autumn to produce those characteristic stately white blooms with startling spiked yellow centre in early summer. Choose a pot to suit the number of rhizomes – between 6in (15cm) for a single swollen root and 10in (25cm) for up to five. Fill the base with drainage crocks before topping up with compost (J.I.P. No. 2). Set the rhizomes 2in (5cm) deep in the compost, firm and water. Stand pots outside in a sheltered spot until the middle of September – later if the weather is mild. Move indoors before the first frost.

This is an ideal time to plant freesias for flowering in mid- and late winter. Their branching sprays of sweetly scented blooms in a range of yellows, whites, pinks and purples are a real treat. Plant six corms about 2in (5cm) apart in a 6in (15cm) pot filled with potting compost. Cover with compost so that each corm is an inch or so deep. Water sparingly at first, increasing rations as growth develops. Freesias, too, can be left outside until frosts threaten. With mid-autumn comes just about the last chance to start freesias.

In late autumn, try potting up a few crowns of lily-of-the-valley for their arching flower stems of dainty white bell-flowers. Keep them just frost-free for an early display to brighten up winter rooms. Pot about twelve good-sized crowns in a 6in (15cm) pot with a potting compost. Provide plenty of drainage.

Lift and pot up roots of Christmas rose, *Helleborous niger*, to get early blooms – perhaps even on Christmas day. Don't put them straight into a warm greenhouse, though. Make a temporary stop for a few days in a cold frame.

LILIES

Lilies should be potted up singly in 6in (15cm) pots from September onwards. There are basically two methods. One way is to set stem-rooting varieties deep into the pot, leaving plenty of space for top dressings of compost as the plant shoots and produces roots up its stem. Other lilies that do not produce roots from the stem should be potted up like other bulbs. Once potted, keep the pots in a cool place watering sparingly until growth shows.

Some lilies like *Lilium longiflorium* can be gently forced at about 61°F (16°C) when the established bulb will produce a flowerbud. Water and feed little and often until colour shows in the bud.

Bulbs

Early autumn is the time to buy in hippeastrums for mid-winter flowering. The sizeable bulbs need a large pot, 6in (15cm) often being necessary. Fill the pot with potting compost, then excavate a small depression to take the bulb so that it sits two-thirds into the compost. Water sparingly until growth becomes apparent, keeping it in a light, draught-proof spot. Maintain the temperature at around 59°F (15°C). Water well as the flowerbud emerges to be followed by dark green strap-shaped leaves.

In early autumn, there is also still time to pot up your lachenalias (Cape cowslips) for their colourful bell-like blooms from early winter onwards. Space six bulbs in a 6in (15cm) pot and cover with 1in (2.5cm) of compost. Place in a cool and ventilated greenhouse or frame.

Pot up narcissus such as 'Soleil d'Or' and 'Paperwhite' for early winter flowering. You can pot up prepared bulbs for forcing. Select firm, healthy bulbs and plant them in large pots or decorative bowls filled with bulb fibre. Do not plant them too deep, though; keep their necks just above the compost surface. Water and then plunge the pots in peat and treat in the same way as daffodils.

It's also worth potting up some of the spring-flowering bulbs purchased for the garden to be brought on early in the greenhouse. This will fill that colour gap before the first of the spring bulbs show in the garden. Try crocus, tulips, daffodils, chionodoxa, erithroniums, snowdrops, *Iris reticulata*, mascari and many more.

RESTING

Tuberous begonias will now be starting to turn yellow to prepare for their winter rest. Reduce watering, allowing the compost to dry out. Place dry tubers in a cool, dry place until spring.

Gloxinias and hippeastrums can be treated in a similar fashion to begonias, except they prefer to be left in their pots during the resting stage. Hippeastrums will need repotting about every three years.

Don't bother keeping gloxinia tubers once they've reached three years old.

PRICKING OUT

Prick out sowings of half-hardy annuals when they are large enough into 3½in (9cm) pots then place in a light, but cool, spot in a greenhouse or frame to get established. Water sparingly and open ventilators whenever weather permits. Earlier sowings which are now well established will need to be pinched out to produce sturdy potted specimens.

Rapidly developing cyclamen will also need pricking out individually into 3½in (9cm) pots as they become too big for the seedtray. Grow on at a temperature of around 59°F (15°C). Feed young growing plants of cyclamen, clarkia, schizanthus, cinerarias and primulas with a weak feed containing plenty of potash.

Plant hippeastrums in autumn for midwinter flowering. The presence of an extra shoot indicates that a daughter bulb is forming.

DAFFODILS

There is nothing better during a dull winter day than to grace the living room with a supply of beautiful daffodils. It is easy to achieve, but often forgotten.

1. Purchase bulbs that have been specially prepared for forcing. If you select containers without drainage holes then it is important to use proprietary bulb fibre if the compost is to remain sweet.

2. Check that the compost is moist, but not too wet. Fill a container with compost to the level of the base of each bulb.

3. Space bulbs around the container – do not 'screw' them in – and then fill in gaps with more compost. Don't fill the container with compost and then push the bulbs in.

4. Cover the bulbs so that their necks are just visible, then place them in a cool spot in the dark to encourage root production and prevent the shoot breaking too early. The traditional way of achieving this is to plunge the containers into a deep bed of peat outside (although under the bed in a cool, spare room would do).

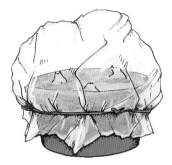

5. Cover in polythene to keep the worst of the weather off, but check that the pots don't get too dry. Check once a week or so too if watering is necessary.

6. When shoots are about 1in (2.5cm) high, retrieve the bulbs from their dark storage place and bring them in to a cool greenhouse. Space young plants on greenhouse staging so that they receive as much light as possible. Water sparingly.

❀ If you forget to plant your daffodil bulbs in early autumn, you can still plant some of the dwarf varieties in late autumn for an early spring show.

FORCING VEGETABLES

In late autumn, dig up chicory roots from sowings made last spring when the larger leaves have died down leaving just the immature heart leaves. Remove sideshoots and cut back foliage to within 1in (2.5cm) of the root. Select roots with at least 1in (2.5cm) crowns, but no larger than 2in (5cm) and pot up three in a 6in (15cm) pot filled with sandy loam-based compost. The remaining roots which are useful for forcing should be stored in a cool, but frost-free place. Pot up a batch every couple of weeks for a continuous supply of crisp subtle-flavoured chicons all winter long. To force chicons it is important to exclude light; this is usually achieved by inverting an empty 6in (15cm) pot on top of the potted roots. Maintain a temperature of around 54°F (12°C) to have succulent shoots in about four weeks. Cooler temperatures just mean a longer forcing period. Cut chicons when 4–6in (10–15cm) long. A root cannot be forced more than once.

Rhubarb crowns for forcing can also be lifted and left to get frosted on the soil surface. Box up crowns in a crate filled with moist peat and cover in black polythene to keep the light out. Check once a week or so to see the compost remains moist.

WATERING, FEEDING AND HEATING

With most plants, watering and feeding should gradually be reduced as growth rates slow down and plants go into dormancy for the winter. Give them just sufficient water to prevent wilting. Although you may have removed the greenhouse shading, be prepared to use temporary shading on those days of uncharacteristically warm weather that sometimes occurs in early autumn.

Flowers

Water and feed developing freesias, lachenalias, lilies and cyclamen. Autumn-flowering chrysanthemums in pots that were stood outside for the summer should be brought inside at the beginning of mid-autumn. Check over the plants for pests and diseases before bringing them inside. Maintain a minimum temperature of 55°F (13°C).

Keep pots of lily-of-the-valley in a cool, but frost-free, greenhouse or frame through late autumn and early winter bringing them into a warm greenhouse or room in mid-winter. Watering should be carried out with utmost care. Do not splash leaves or tubers and crowns, otherwise you run the risk of encouraging botrytis. Liquid feed actively growing pot plants every ten days or so and try to maintain good light to prevent plants becoming leggy.

Fruit and Vegetables

In early autumn, lift melons up to give them maximum light and protect them from cold snaps at night with horticultural fleece. Keep the atmosphere dry and reduce watering.

As the first grapes start to ripen steps must be taken to reduce the risk of fruit splitting. Rapid changes in temperature and high humidity are thought to be the main culprits, provided adequate water has been given through the life of the crop.

The sweet-scented Nicotiana (tobacco plant) blooms from mid-summer to early autumn. Grow in the shade if you want to see flowers open during the day.

Prevent cucumbers from touching the soil or any wet areas by placing a piece of wood or a pad underneath them.

Damping down should, therefore, be carried out in the morning and a roof vent should be left open at night to lower humidity and slow the early morning heating effects of the sun. Prevent uneven watering by giving the border a thick mulch.

Check the bunches for diseases and pests throughout early autumn, removing affected fruit as soon as they are noticed. Avoid touching the grapes.

Ventilate peaches and nectarines freely on dry days to ripen the current year's wood and keep the temperature down. Don't let the temperature drop too low at night, though.

Newly potted, rooted strawberry runners will be filling out their pots as they become established. Stand them in a sunny, sheltered spot. Spray the leaves each day and water as necessary.

Feed and water aubergines and sweet peppers as necessary.

The watering of tomatoes is still critical at this time but shouldn't be quite as time consuming as it was in late summer.

PINCHING AND PRUNING

Keep on top of your tipping back of new shoots arising from the grape vine. They must be cut back to the first leaf, otherwise they'll take over the greenhouse. Tendrils will also develop at an alarming rate and need removing as soon as you notice them.

Leaf fall usually occurs in mid-autumn and spells the time for the winter pruning of grape vines. Make sure the vine is completely dormant before you start, by cooling the greenhouse right down through generous ventilation. A dormant vine avoids the problem of bleeding shoots after pruning.

Cut back all the current season's growth to within two buds unless it is required to replace older rods (stems) or to extend existing ones. All supporting wires should be cleaned up and replaced where necessary.

HARVESTING

Ripening and harvesting of tomatoes will continue throughout early autumn in the greenhouse. If night temperatures can be kept up then fruit can be

---

DISBUDDING

It is important to disbud chrysanthemums if you require large single blooms. Remove all the lateral buds on the leaf axils leading to the terminal bud which is left to produce the bloom. Spray varieties need to have only the terminal bud removed.

Tomatoes continue to ripen throughout early autumn, but if space is very short you can harvest the last green fruit and allow it to ripen in the kitchen.

harvested the following month too. However, there will be a great demand for greenhouse space towards mid-autumn with all the tender perennials in pots needing protection, so it is a good idea to take the last harvest of fruit by then.

All fruit that are starting to turn colour should be picked off and placed on a tray on the windowsill to ripen. Make a winter stock of green tomato chutney with the less advanced fruit.

If tomato plants are removed to the compost heap clear up all debris.

Sweet peppers and aubergines should be harvested throughout early autumn. Feed and water as necessary. When the last have been harvested, remove and discard the bare plants.

As grapes colour up they seem ripe for harvesting, but this is not the case. Depending on variety they will need to be left on the vine for at least a couple of weeks and sometimes a lot longer before they are at their best. It takes this time for the sugars to develop in the fruit. Harvesting is as easy as you make it. If you cut each bunch with a stem handling is a lot easier. Once the grapes are fully ripe they can be kept on the vine for several weeks, provided the atmosphere is dry, and the temperature cool (around 45°F; 7°C).

You can keep the fruit of some varieties of grape vine for several weeks after harvesting. 'Lady Downe's Seedling' for instance, will last until mid-winter, though only if the stem is placed in water.

Harvest any remaining peaches and nectarines as they ripen on the fruit trees started into growth late in the spring. Continue to ventilate the greenhouse so that the new wood produced this year becomes fully ripened. Try not to let temperatures fall too low, though.

Harvest frame-grown melons when the skin of the fruit starts to crack around the stem.

OVERWINTERING

Flowers

In mid-autumn, dahlia enthusiasts will want to check over their crop and carefully label, low down on the plant, those worth keeping to produce cuttings next year. This roguing operation is essential to improve the stock. It's also worth colour coding the labels so that the display next year produces the whole range available.

Carefully lift and store dahlia tubers after the first frost has turned the flowerbuds black. Lift them anyway by the end of mid-autumn. Choose a dry spell so that soil is easily removed from the tubers, then cut back the main stem to about 6in (15cm). Dust dry tubers with a fungicidal powder such as 'flowers of sulphur'. Store in boxes filled with a dry peat in a well-shaded, cool, frost-free place; under greenhouse staging is ideal.

Fuchsias to be grown as standards next year should be selected from the crop of rooted cuttings in 3½in (9cm) pots taken earlier this year. Each will need to be caned and tied with string or wire rings. However, if the plants are to be kept growing all winter a temperature of around 50°F (10°C) must be maintained.

By late autumn, chrysanthemums in outdoor beds will be well past their prime and it's time to select stocks for taking cuttings from next year. Carefully label each plant as near to the ground as

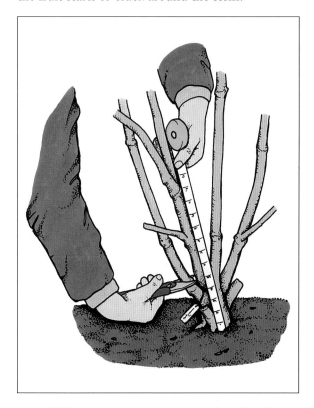

Label dahlias before cutting them back to about 5in (12cm).

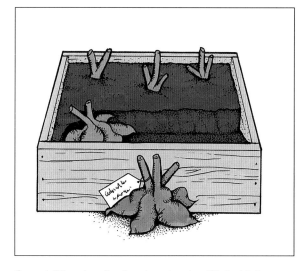

Store dahlia tubers for the winter in a box filled with dry peat.

SAVING MONEY ON TENDER PERENNIALS

Cut back tender perennials like these Pelargoniums.

Box up after cutting back and cover roots with compost.

Tender patio and hanging basket plants, such as marguerites and osteospurmums, are all the rage these days. They soon make colourful long-lasting displays from small plants bought early in the spring. However, if you have a lot of pots and hanging baskets, buying new plants each year can be very expensive. What many gardeners overlook is that most tender perennials are easy to overwinter and can either be planted out again the following year or encouraged to supply cutting material for new plants.

In a warm greenhouse or conservatory, you can keep tender perennials actively growing throughout the winter months so that the plants in spring are larger and even more impressive. Alternatively, you can take cuttings in the autumn and root them overwinter, so the new plants have a head start when planted out after the last frosts in spring. If you heat your greenhouse to keep the frost out you can overwinter tender plants in their original containers.

In an unheated greenhouse or cold frame you can still overwinter plants. To keep them frost free it will be necessary to partition off a small area off the ground in the centre of the greenhouse using bubble polythene. A wooden box on a couple of breeze blocks is ideal. Alternatively, move your cold frame into the greenhouse and use that. If the weather turns exceptionally cold, cover the box with extra insulation such as sheets of bubble polythene, old newspapers or a piece of old carpet.

WHOLE PLANTS

Individual specimens can be potted up and the top growth cut back by two-thirds before being stood on the greenhouse bench over winter. The compost should be kept on the dry side by watering sparingly.

Many specimens, such as geraniums, marguerites and felicias, can be boxed up together. Cut back plants hard – each main stem to 2–4in (5–10cm) of the rootstock – so that they can be crammed into

SAVING MONEY ON TENDER PERENNIALS

Wrap up tender perennials in pots to protect roots.

In really cold weather cover crops with horticultural fleece.

boxes. Cover specimens with a half-and-half mix of compost and sharp sand.

ROOTSTOCKS

Those plants that die back in autumn but need to be kept frost free, such as cannas and dahlias, should be lifted from the border when the foliage dies down, all top-growth removed and the rootball or crown crammed side-by-side into boxes. Cover roots with a half-and-half mix of compost and sharp sand.

CUTTINGS

Although the greenhouse is empty when the tender perennials are put into the greenhouse for the winter, they need to stay protected until after the last frost in spring. By this time your greenhouse will be very short of space. One option is to take cuttings in late summer or early autumn and overwinter these. You can get at least six times as many rooted cuttings in the space taken by a single overwintered plant:

1. Select healthy, non-flowering shoots.
2. Trim to about 3in.
3. Remove lower leaves.
4. Dip in a plant fungicide.
5. Insert six cuttings around the edge of a 3½in (9cm) pot filled with half-and-half mix of compost and sharp sand.
6. Water well and cover pot in a clear polythene bag supported on a wire hoop (do not cover hairy leaved cuttings with polythene).
7. Keep the rooted cuttings cool but frost free and their compost slightly moist. They shouldn't be encouraged to put on any growth until the spring.

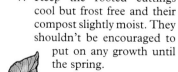

WHAT TO DO IN SPRING

As soon as temperatures rise in early or mid-spring, plants, rootstocks and rooted cuttings will all burst into life. It is essential that you keep an eye on them at this time so you can increase watering as necessary. Pot up cuttings individually into 3½in (9cm) pots and repot specimens in fresh compost. Extra cuttings can be taken now from new shoots to bulk up the number of plants. Plant out all tender perennials after the last frosts.

possible, then lift and cut each stem down to about 4in (10cm). Choose a dry spell to tease soil away from roots, then place in deep boxes filled with peat. Keep these in a cool spot – under staging in a cool greenhouse is ideal – until the next spring.

Chrysanthemums will survive the winter outside in the beds, provided they don't get too wet, but for best results take new cuttings each spring from the overwintered selected stocks.

Peaches and nectarines require a dry cool atmosphere to enable this year's wood to ripen. This may mean turning on heaters on damp, misty days to lower humidity and increase temperature.

Continue to water the new strawberry plants that will now be establishing themselves well on their 6in (15cm) pots. Spray the leaves each sunny morning. Discontinue watering and overhead spraying as soon as the plants start to show signs of going into dormancy. Rotting crowns can be a problem in the cold, wet winter months so it is best to move the plants to a cold frame and ventilate freely. Apply a fungicidal drench as a preventative measure.

Strawberries will remain dormant from around the beginning of late autumn to mid-winter, when they are taken into the greenhouse and started off. If strawberries are in a cold frame they must be kept well ventilated.

WHAT TO OVERWINTER

If space is tight, stick to plants that are expensive to buy or difficult to get hold of:

Begonia
Bidens

Brachycome
Busy Lizzie

Calceolaria
Cineraria
Coleus
Diasica
Dahlia
Felicia
Gazania
Glechoma
Heliotrope
Helichrysum
Lantana
Lobelia
Lotus
Marguerite
Osteospurmum
Pansy
Pelargonium
 (geranium)
Plectranthus
Scaevola
Verbena
Viola

Geranium *'Hollywood Star'*.

CHAPTER 9

Winter

The coldest winter weather doesn't usually arrive until mid-winter so early winter is usually the last chance to protect those not-so hardy specimens in the garden.

GENERAL MANAGEMENT

Early winter

Cautious watering and ventilation should be continued. Shut down ventilators at night, opening them only on sunny days. Again, maintain a minimum temperature of 45°F (7°C) at night and around 54°F (12°C) during the day for the majority of greenhouse plants.

Wash down the greenhouse and remove all debris, if not already done.

It is probably worth insulating any greenhouse that is heated during the winter months. Deciding what type of greenhouse insulation to buy depends to a large extent on the temperature lift required: that is, the difference between inside and outside temperatures.

The simplest form of insulation is polythene sheet. This can be attached to the greenhouse structure using pins on wood or special clips on aluminium. The idea is to create a still, insulative layer of about ½in (1.25cm) between the side of the glass and the polythene sheet. If sheets are not properly joined together or tend to move with the breeze then much of the insulation effect is lost.

For very leaky greenhouses it's best to plump for the more expensive, but more effective, bubble polythene. However, this again must be put up properly to gain the maximum benefit. This type of plastic double glazing does reduce light levels a little, but not too drastically.

One of the major restrictions to greenhouse gardening in the winter months is light. If you heat your greenhouse up too much there is a real chance of plants producing weak spindly growth because of lack of light. This can be a particular hazard with early sown crops like pelargoniums and tomatoes.

Bubble plastic makes a very effective insulator.

Many lamps are available for the greenhouse to supplement existing light and to extend day length.

Mid-winter

Mid-winter is usually the coldest time of the year and this can curtail gardening activities unless there is a greenhouse to hand. A heated greenhouse can be an inspiration of colour with primulas, calceolarias, cinerarias and cyclamen all brightening up an otherwise dull garden. Those with enough space for an Indian azalea or arum lily will be in for a treat at this time.

A careful balance must be maintained between heating, watering and ventilation during the tricky first few months of the year.

Watering cyclamen must be carried out with meticulous care, making certain that the foliage and more particularly, the crowns of pot plants are not soaked. This will cause rot to set in and the dramatic collapse of foliage. It is best, therefore, to water from below during the early part of the day – soaking each plant thoroughly, then not returning to water again until the compost is quite dry. Do not overwater.

Incidentally, where a cyclamen plant does collapse it is worth checking the corm and root system for vine weevil larvae, which eat the fleshy roots. Where vine weevils are discovered throw out the affected plant and treat others with an insecticide or biological control (*see* 'Controlling Pests Without Chemicals').

Skilful ventilation is the secret to keeping fuel bills down. During bright, sunny, windless days open the ridge vents to allow a little air circulation within the greenhouse. On breezy days open the ridge vent on the leeward side of the greenhouse. Don't ventilate during very windy weather. When the vents are open it is worth shutting them a couple of hours before dusk to capture some of the sun's energy and give the heaters a head start.

All heaters and automatic ventilators should be checked regularly at this time of year. Paraffin

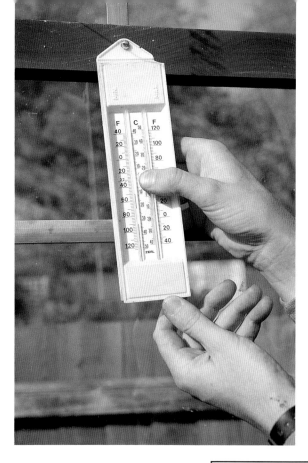

Maximum/minimum thermometers are essential greenhouse equipment.

for botrytis, grey mould fungus, because this can play havoc in the greenhouse at this time of year. Also peruse all your flowering plants on a regular basis, removing dead flowers promptly.

Daffodils, tulips and hyacinths can be brought inside from the plunge beds (sited in a sheltered spot in the garden) to maintain the continuity of flowering plants in the greenhouse. Don't send them into shock, though, by making this transfer too rapid; it is best to put them in a cold frame for a couple of days first.

Cold greenhouses that are standing empty can be given the full clean-up treatment – scrubbing down the greenhouse structure and sterilizing soil and compost (*see also* Chapter 8). Any recent vacated or forgotten pots and seedtrays should be cleaned and stored in readiness for the busy sowing season ahead.

heaters, in particular, need regular maintenance and filling, but don't be tempted to neglect the less demanding heating systems since any type can fail.

Maximum/minimum thermometers are an essential aid to the greenhouse grower, giving an accurate assessment of the temperature of the previous night. Use this information to adjust your heating and ventilation balance.

General maintenance of the greenhouse should not be neglected either; replace cracked or broken panes of glass promptly. Check insulation for gaps or sagging particularly in the roof sections – and fix where necessary.

Check all overwintered stock of cuttings taken during the autumn. Remove and compost any yellowing leaves. Watch out

WINTER CHECKS

1. Check all nuts and bolts and tighten any that have worked loose.

2. Check that all vents close snugly. Replace any broken panes.

TIP

Many house plants will now be suffering from the low light levels that occur indoors at this time of year. So it is worth bringing them into a heated greenhouse on a rota basis to keep them happy.

Schefflera *'Umbrella Tree'*.

Late Winter

In most years, late winter is a calm, dry and cold time. Greenhouse heaters are often working flat out day and night to maintain the required temperature but still the heated greenhouse will reward us with a bounty of colour throughout the period. Again many primulas, calceolarias, cinerarias and cyclamen are in bloom. Early sowings can be made now in a heated greenhouse, but if you delay until early spring next month, you will save money on heating costs.

Hygiene is important at this time of year when ventilation is limited and temperatures are down. Systematically purge the greenhouse of dead and dying leaves and promptly remove flowers that are past their prime. Check for pests and diseases now to prevent them getting an early foothold. Spray as necessary.

Ventilation is of paramount importance but once again, it should only occur during calm, sunny spells. Don't be tempted to open up the vents on dank, misty days or when there's a keen wind blowing that might cause a drop in temperature inside the greenhouse. Automatic vents can be a problem at this time of the year because they tend to open too wide and remain ajar right into the evening, losing valuable heat right at the end of the day.

Watering must be given as and when necessary – a great deal more will be required by plants in active growth on bright, sunny days. Most winter watering is best done from below by standing the pot plant in a tray and then adding water or immersing the pot up to its rim in a bowl of water

LATE WINTER QUICK-REFERENCE CHECKLIST

❁ Keep on top of greenhouse hygiene; wash and sterilize pots and seedtrays.
❁ Continue careful heating, watering and ventilation.
❁ Check insulation.

FLOWERS

❁ Sow half-hardy annuals and perennials.
❁ Sow sweet peas, bedding dahlias and several greenhouse pot plants.
❁ Take cuttings from chrysanthemums and carnations.
❁ Plant achimene tubers.
❁ Prune greenhouse fuchsias, bougainvilleas, gardenias and overwintered pelargoniums.

VEGETABLES

❁ Sow early melons and cucumbers for raising in a heated greenhouse.
❁ Sow broad beans and early peas if not done in autumn.
❁ Sow early lettuce, cauliflower, cabbage and Brussels sprouts.

FRUIT

❁ Hand pollinate early peaches, nectarines and apricots as well as early vines.
❁ Bring potted strawberry runners inside.

Opuntia subulata.

for a few minutes. Whichever method is used, a pot plant must be given an opportunity to drain fully before being returned to its position on the staging.

The weather dictates most activities in the greenhouse and none more so than heating. The choice of cleaning, filling and trimming the wick of paraffin heaters, makes them unpopular these days. In addition they have to be lit every time the temperature threatens to plummet. Other forms of heating need less maintenance and are often thermostatically controlled to make them more fuel efficient. But even these systems should be checked regularly just in case something goes wrong. After all, it only takes one penetrating frost to wipe out all your early starters.

It is not worth heating the entire greenhouse just to get a few garden crops off to an early start. It is far better to invest in a soil-warming cable and install it in a partitioned-off section of the greenhouse. Soil-warming cables are cheap to run and provided there is already an electricity supply are easy to install (*see also* Greenhouse Equipment, Chapter 3). The heat produced by soil-warming cables raises the temperature of the compost in pots and seedtrays placed on top – this speeds germination and encourages root development. If you intend to install one buy it now to realize maximum benefit from your investment.

Check through the stock of pots and seedtrays to make sure they are ready for use as well as ensuring there are sufficient labels for the coming season. Sit down and run through the sowing programme for the weeks ahead to check there will be continuity of supply through the season. Use rubber bands to group packets of seeds that can be sown at the same time under the same or very similar conditions. This highlights those requiring special treatment. Make a checklist for all these jobs otherwise something is bound to be forgotten.

PROPAGATION

Flowers

Carnations and Chrysanthemums
Perpetual-flowering carnations can be propagated in early winter from cuttings. Do not select shoots from too near the top or the base of the plant. Take 3in (7.5cm) cuttings, snapped cleanly out of the parent plant. Trim them up using a sharp knife and dip the cut end in hormone rooting powder. Stick cuttings around the edge of a 3½in (9cm) pot filled with gritty compost.

Chrysanthemums can be propagated as soon as suitable material is being produced by the stocks.

Decorative varieties that were cut back to within 6in (15cm) and overwintered in the greenhouse will be producing fresh young shoots by mid-winter.

1. Select basal shoots around 3in (7.5cm) long that are not too drawn. Some varieties are a little slow in producing basal shoots, so encourage them by adding a few handfuls of fresh compost around the stool and increasing the temperature a little. Wait until shoots are around 4in (10cm) long before taking cuttings to leave a ½–1in (1–2.5cm) snag that will rapidly produce another set of shoots.
2. Use a sharp knife to remove basal shoots from the stool, then trim the cutting to just below a leaf joint.

3. Dip cut ends in hormone rooting powder.
4. Insert prepared cuttings either singly in the cells of a modular seedtray or two per 3½in (9cm) pot filled with a gritty cuttings compost with a layer of silver sand on top to aid drainage. Where many cuttings are being taken, insert them 2in (5cm) apart in boxes filled with compost. Water well.

Cuttings will not require watering again, but it is worth spraying the tops with water to prevent them from flagging too much. Although heat is not required, best results are obtained if the cuttings are placed in a propagator and given a little bottom heat. Rooting should occur within two or three weeks.

Perpetual-flowering carnations can be propagated from cuttings from early winter. They will produce sideshoots from nodes right up the stem. When taking cuttings, avoid shoots close to the top of the plant as well as those around the base.

1. As with the decorative chrysanthemums, take 3in (7.5cm) cuttings, which should be snapped cleanly out from the leaf joint of the parent plant.
2. Using a sharp knife, trim up the base, dip it in hormone powder and shake off excess.
3. Push cuttings into a modular seedtray filled with cuttings compost, or around the edge of 3½in (9cm) pot. Water well.
4. Place in a propagator and give a little bottom heat, 61°F (16°C) if possible. Rooting will take place within a few weeks provided the tops are prevented from wilting.

Cuttings can be taken from chrysanthemums and carnations throughout the winter.

Dahlias
Border dahlias can be increased in late winter.

1. Select some healthy tubers that have been stored over winter in a cool, dark, frost-free place. These can now be boxed in a moist peat and sand mix with their crowns clear of the surface.
2. Place in a warm, light position so the tubers swell and start to produce shoots suitable for taking cuttings. You should aim for a temperature of around 61°F (16°C) for a good supply of short-jointed, fresh green shoots.
3. When new shoots are 3–4in (7.5–10cm) long, cut them off with a sharp knife, leaving a ½in (1.25cm) stump from which the new shoots will develop.
4. Then treat as softwood cuttings (*see* Propagation, Chapter 5).

Fuchsias
Where side shoots of overwintered plants are long enough, they can be used as cutting material in early winter.

Trim each cutting just below a leaf node using a sharp knife and remove lower leaves. Dip the end in hormone rooting powder and insert into a gritty

SOWING IDEAS

Name	Germ. Temp. (°C)	Germ. Time (wks)	Plant Out	Comments
Althea rosea (hollyhock)	13–15	2–3	Mid-/late spring	Large pink flowers from mid-summer to early autumn on rigid stems. Light green hairy leaves.
Antirrhinum majus (snapdragon) e.g. 'Coronette' (mixed), 'Magic Carpet' (pastel)	16–18	1–3	early spring to early summer	Flowers from mid-summer to early autumn in a variety of colours. Look for rust-resistant varieties.
Calceolaria 'Anytime' series	18–21	2–3	Potgrown	As the name suggests can be sown any time for a show four months later.
Canna (Indian shot)	21–24	3–8	late spring	Soak seed 24hrs before sowing. Blooms mid-summer to early autumn.
Lathyrus odotatus (sweet pea)	13–18	2–3	mid-/late spring	Scented flowers in pink, white and purple are produced from early summer to early autumn.
Lobelia erinus compacta	18–21	2–3	mid-/late spring	Sow on surface. Many varieties with flowers varying in shades of blue set off against dainty foliage. Blooms late spring to early autumn.
Pelargonium (geranium) e.g. 'Multibloom' (series), 'Sensation' (series), 'Orange Appeal'	21–24	1–3	late spring	Continuous display from early summer to early autumn, striking pinks, powerful reds and subtle whites.
Salvia patens	18–21	2–3	late spring	Provides a display of azure blue claw-shaped flowers on 2in (5cm)spikes in late summer early autumn.
Salvia splendens	18–21	2–3	late spring	Best known as summer bedding with its blazing red spike from mid-summer to early autumn.
Sinningia speciosa (gloxinia)	18–24	2–3	Potgrown	Wider range of spectacular colours from late spring to late summer.
Verbena × hybrida	18–21	3–4	late spring	Many varieties available giving a wide range of sparkling colours from early summer to early autumn.

ANNUALS:

Name	Germ. Temp. (°C)	Germ. Time (wks)	Plant Out	Comments
Alyssum maritimum e.g. 'Snow Crystals' (white), 'Wonderland' (mixed and single colours)	10–15	1–2	mid-spring	Transplant either singly or in clumps. Blooms from early summer to late autumn.
Celosia plumosa 'Century Mixed'	18–21	2–3	late spring/ early summer	Good pot plants and bedding if hardened off carefully. Blooms all summer.

Name	Germ. Temp. (°C)	Germ. Time (wks)	Plant Out	Comments
Gerbera jamesonii (Transvaal daisy)	18–21	2–3	late spring	Fabulous coloured large blooms on strong stems from late spring to late summer.
Latherus adoratus (sweet pea)	13–18	1–3	mid-/late spring	Scented flowers in pink, white and purple are produced from early summer to early autumn.
Mattiola incana 'Mixed' (East Lothian stocks)	15–18	1–2	mid-/late spring	Flowers appear early and mid-summer on 12in (30cm) spikes in colours ranging from white to purple.
Nicotiana alata (tobacco plant)	18–21	2–3	late spring	Blooms from mid-summer to early autumn producing a sweet scent. Grow in shade if you want to see flowers open during the day.

PERENNIALS:

Name	Germ. Temp. (°C)	Germ. Time (wks)	Plant Out	Comments
Althea rosea (hollyhock)	13–15	2–3	late spring	Large single or double pink flowers from mid-summer to early autumn on rigid stems.
Antirrhinum majus (snapdragon) e.g. 'Coronette' (mixed), 'Magic Carpet' (pastel)	16–18	2–3	mid-spring/ early summer	Flowers from mid-summer to early autumn. Look for rust-resistant varieties.
Calceolaria e.g. 'Anytime Series'	18–21	2–3	Potgrown	Sow on the surface to get spectacular show just four months later. Many colours.
Canna (Indian shot)	21–24	3–8	late spring	Soak seed 24hrs before sowing. Many colours from mid-summer to early summer.
Catananche caerulea (Cupid's Dart)	13–15	2–3	late spring	Summer flowers of brilliant sky-blue. Good as cut flowers in water.
Chrysanthemum parthenium	13–15	1–2	mid-/late spring	Yellow and white varieties produced freely from mid-summer to early autumn
Lobelia erinus compacta	18–21	2–3	mid-/late spring	Sow on surface. Blooms from late spring to early autumn. Seeds poisonous if eaten.
Pelargonium (geranium) e.g. 'Multibloom' (series), 'Sensation' (series), 'Orange Appeal'	21–24	1–3	late spring	Much loved bedding and pot plant that produces its colours in pink, powerful reds and subtle whites.
Salvia patens	18–21	2–3	late spring	Late summer to early autumn produces azure blue claw-shaped flowers on a spike 2in (5cm) tall.
Slavia splendens	18–21	2–3	late spring	Produces its blazing red spike from mid-summer to early autumn. Very popular bedding plant.

Name	Germ. Temp. (°C)	Germ. Time (wks)	Plant Out	Comments
Sinnigia speciosa (gloxinia)	18–24	2–3	Pot grown	Sow on surface. Range of spectacular colours produced from late spring to late summer.
Tropaeolum perefrinum (Canary creeper)	13–18	2	Mid-/late spring	Fast growing creeper that produces lots of pretty yellow flowers all summer.
Verbena × hybrida	18–21	3–4	late spring	Flowers early summer to early autumn with the large number of varieties producing wide range of colours.

cuttings compost. Maintain a temperature of around 61°F (16°C) for speedy rooting.

Seed

Sowing starts at a gentle pace in mid-winter with half a dozen or so different plants. Many will germinate admirably with a temperature around 59–64°F (15–18°C) – most economically provided by a propagator – although pelargonium, salvia and gloxinia prefer a couple of degrees more warmth.

Early sowings are particularly prone to attacks by fungus diseases. It is, therefore, worth making these sowings thinner than normal to allow better air circulation between the seedlings. Also water with a fungicide such as 'Cheshunt Compound' to give protection. Don't be tempted to go overboard with these early sowings because they will have to remain in the greenhouse until late spring when space is always at a premium.

With the onset of late winter, sowing begins in earnest, so get yourself organized. Make sure there is enough compost for the coming weeks.

MAIL-ORDERED SEED

Ordered seed will be arriving from the seedhouses from early winter. They must be stored in a dry, frost-free place to keep them in top condition. There is still time to make fresh orders for seeds and young plants by mail order. Remember though that many suppliers of seedlings and tiny plants have a last orders deadline in early spring.

SOWING SWEET PEAS STEP-BY-STEP

Sweet peas can be sown in late winter, but those destined for the local flower show can be sown in early winter provided they are given heat.

1. Lay blotting or tissue paper in a shallow dish and soak with water.

2. Lay the seed on the paper, then cover with another sheet of wet paper. The seeds will soon swell and produce a radicle within three or four days. Any seed that doesn't respond by swelling should be nicked to encourage water absorption.

3. Place germinated seed individually in special sweet-pea tubes, about ½in (1.25cm) deep in a peat-based potting compost (or J.I.P. No 2), or sow three or four seeds per 3½in (9cm) pot.

4. Protect against mice feasting on the seed by covering sown pots with a sheet of glass.

Alternatively, soak seed in warm water for twenty-four hours before sowing to speed germination. Sow three or four seeds about ½in (1.25cm) deep in 3½in (9cm) pots. Water thoroughly and maintain a temperature of around 61°F (16°C).

Many half-hardy annuals can be sown in late winter, destined to decorate beds and borders throughout the garden. Take care not to sow too much at this stage, otherwise you may run out of space for later sowings.

Bedding dahlias need to be sown during late winter or early spring in a seedtray at a temperature of 61°F (16°C). Germination will quickly occur and new seedlings should be potted up individually as soon as they can be handled safely. The dwarf 'Coltness Hybrids', 'Rigoletto' and 'Redskin' are tried and trusted varieties.

Vegetables and Fruit

In mid-winter, a range of early vegetables can be sown, the most important of which is the early tomato. You will need either plenty of room or not intend growing much else if you embark on cultivating early tomatoes in a heated greenhouse for first harvest in early summer. Tomatoes need consistent heat, so a reliable well-regulated heating system is necessary to give a minimum temperature of 64°F (18°C) from seedling stage until established. Temperatures can then be reduced gradually to 55°F (13°C) at night until plants are ready for planting out, when a minimum of 50°F (10°C) should be aimed for. If your heating system is not capable of maintaining such high temperatures early on or is not 100 per cent reliable then it would be wise to delay sowing until early spring, or buy in plants in mid-spring. Producing early tomatoes is an expensive gamble.

1. Sow very thinly. Tomato seed is large enough to sow singly so space six rows of four across a standard seedtray.
2. Cover the seed with ¼in (6mm) of compost, water thoroughly, then place a sheet of glass and a newspaper over the seedtray. Maintain a temperature of 70°F (21°C) for quick germination, but 59–86°F (15–30°C) would do.

   Check the seedtray each day and wipe condensation off the glass to prevent drips falling onto the compost and emerging seedlings.
3. Remove the glass and newspaper as soon as the first seedlings break through, then put the seedtray in a light position to prevent the

Sow tomato seed individually, well spaced.

seedlings from becoming drawn. Keep out of direct sunlight.
4. When the first true leaves are expanding, lift the seedlings carefully and pot up individually into 3½in (9cm) pots. Do not handle them by their stems but hold one seedleaf between finger and thumb while supporting the root system with a small dibber or plant label. Discard any odd looking or small seedlings since they invariably both develop and fruit poorly.

The earliest crops of dwarf French beans can also be sown in mid-winter and can be grown in the greenhouse borders before maincrop tomatoes put them in the shade. Varieties like 'Masterpiece' and 'The Prince' are often recommended. Sow 1in (2.5cm) deep during the latter half of mid-winter in peat pots in a temperature of 61°F (16°C). Water well. Plant out in the greenhouse border 6in (15cm) apart when roots start to show through the pot. Alternatively, sow five seeds in a 6in (15cm) pot filled with a peat-based potting compost (or J.I.P. No. 2).

Large onions and leeks for showing can be obtained if they are sown during mid-winter, in heat under glass, ready to be planted out as sturdy seedlings as the weather improves in late spring. Maintain a temperature of 61°F (16°C) for best results, with seed sown individually in the cells of a modular seedtray or thinly in a standard seedtray filled with sowing compost.

To maintain a continuity of firm, crisp heads of lettuce in spring, sow the variety 'Ricardo' direct into the greenhouse border. From sowing to harvesting takes just three or four months in a heated greenhouse and up to five months in an unheated one.

Lettuce can be sown and harvested throughout the winter.

In late winter, the first crops of outdoor lettuce can be sown in a temperature of 55°F (13°C). Varieties such as 'Avondefiance', 'Little Gem' and 'Great Lakes' should be sown ¼in (6mm) deep into peat blocks or fibre pots for best results. Once germinated, harden off in a cold frame and plant outside from mid-spring onwards provided the weather is suitable. Alternatively make further sowings of the 'Iceberg' type lettuce, 'Marmer', direct into the greenhouse border where the temperature is kept above freezing for harvesting in late spring.

Bright scarlet radishes like the variety F1 'Cyros' can be sown in succession from mid-autumn to mid-winter in an unheated greenhouse to provide a much welcomed supply of fresh salad in early spring.

For an early crop of cucumbers, sow in late winter, provided there is a good heating system that is 100 per cent reliable. Only one sowing is necessary since the plants will, with luck, crop the entire season if given the correct treatment. Try an all-female variety such as 'Flamingo' which can yield for several months. Select 3½in (9cm) pots and sow two seeds per pot as for melons. Cucumbers require a gemination temperature of around 24°C and can be emerging in just a week or so. Remove the weakest seedling from each pot.

If you were unable to sow broad beans last autumn they can be sown in late winter in pots in the greenhouse. Use 3½in (9cm) deep in a peat-based seed compost. No heat is required – just frost-free nights. Even a well-insulated frame would do. Harden off in early spring for planting out in mid-spring.

Sow early pea varieties such as 'Little Marvel' and 'Early Onward' if the mid-autumn sowing directly outside was missed. Sow in pots. A novel method is to sow in a compost-filled gutter pipe. Sow two rows 2–3in (5–7.5cm) apart with seed staggered down the pipe. A temperature of around 55°F (13°C) will be sufficient.

The slow-to-germinate aubergine (egg plant) should be sown under glass during late winter. Sow singly into peat pots filled with sowing compost and maintain a temperature of at least 64°F (18°C).

If you have a heated greenhouse it's a good time to make first sowings of cauliflower; cabbage and Brussels sprout. Again a temperature of around 55°F (13°C) or slightly above is ideal. Sow seed very thinly in a seedtray or individually in a modular seedtray using a sowing compost.

Start to harden off autumn-sown early-summer cauliflowers for planting out in early spring.

Melon seed needs to be sown in succession from late winter until late spring if you want plants cropping all summer. Early sowings will need a well-heated greenhouse for the first few months. The easy to grow 'Sweetheart' that produces sweet and aromatic fruit and the productive 'Ogen' with its delicate pale green flesh are two varieties worth considering.

1. Sow two seeds in a 3½in (9cm) pot filled with compost. Place each flat seed on its edge to prevent rotting, about ½in (1.25cm) deep using a small dibber.
2. Place pots in a tray and water. Allow the pots to drain, then lay a sheet of glass and a piece of paper over the top and maintain a temperature of at least 64°F (18°C) but preferably 70°F (21°C). (The glass will also protect the seed from avaricious mice that find melon seeds irresistible.)
3. Check the pots each day and remove the glass and paper as soon as the first seedlings appear.

POTTING, PLANTING AND STARTING

Flowers

Chrysanthemum and carnation cuttings taken earlier in the season should have rooted by mid-winter. Pot them up individually into 3½in (9cm) pots filled with a peat-based compost (or J.I.P. No. 1), which will prevent their growth from being checked by lack of nutrients in the cuttings compost. Take great care when teasing roots apart to prevent damage.

Take further cuttings from carnations, and place all recently potted plants in a light, but cool spot out of direct sunlight.

Cyclamen seedlings sown in autumn can also be potted up.

Hippeastrums that flowered last year can be brought into growth in mid-winter. Every two or three years they will need re-potting. Using a peat-based compost (or J.I.P. No 2) in a 6in (15cm) pot, plant one bulb so that it is about two-thirds buried. In subsequent years just remove the top layer of compost and replace it with fresh. Aim for a temperature around 15°C and the bulb will soon produce the flat green tips of the leaves,

quickly followed (and sometimes preceded) by a plump flowerbud. Water and feed as soon as growth is apparent.

Gloxinia tubers can also be started off now if you can keep a temperature of about 70°F (21°C). Place tubers in a tray or box filled with moist peat to encourage the swelling buds into growth. Then pot each tuber up singly into 6in (15cm) pots filled with potting compost such as John Innes potting compost No. 2. It is probably better to choose loam-based compost because the plants get top heavy.

Once potted, grow plants in a lightly shaded position in a temperature of about 64°F (18°C). Keep well watered and feed once a fortnight.

Standard fuchsias that have filled their 5in (12.5cm) pot and grown beyond the supporting split cane will be ready for moving into an 8in (20cm) pot. Replace the split cane with a 4ft (1.2m) long bamboo and pinch back sideshoots to the first pair of leaves.

In late winter, pot up achimenes grub-like tubers to get an impressive display in several glorious colours. Six or eight tubers can easily be accommo-dated in a 6in (15cm) pot and will give a good display. Either plant about 1in (2.5cm) deep direct in the pot using a proprietary potting compost or lay the tubers on the surface and give them a slight covering of compost. Once sprouted they can be potted up. Whatever the method used, the tubers should be watered well and kept in a temperature of 61°F (16°C) until signs of growth can be clearly seen.

Hippeastrums can be started into growth in mid-winter.

Standard fuchsia.

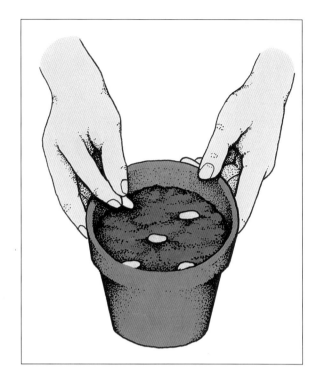

In late winter, pot up the grub-like achimene tubers. Cover with a 1in (2.5cm) of compost.

Subsequently the plants should be fed at fortnightly intervals. If you have enough tubers it is a nice idea to stagger the starting dates of each potful to get an extended flowering display.

Store seed potatoes in a box until they have sprouted. Then plant out or pot up.

Vegetables and Fruit

Seed potatoes become available in mid-winter. Select healthy medium-sized tubers and set them in trays with the plumpest eyes uppermost. Keep in a frost-free position (under staging is ideal) – where they'll begin to sprout (chit). Also keep them out of reach of mice.

It is possible to plant a few tubers of early varieties such as 'Maris Bard' and 'Suttons Foremost' into large pots where they'll grow and produce a plateful of succulent early potatoes in mid- and late spring. A large pot or tub is required (12in; 30cm) diameter) for forcing early potatoes:

1. Cover the base with a 2in (5cm) layer of compost, then arrange three healthy, chitted tubers on the surface and cover these with a further 2in (5cm) of compost.
2. Water well and keep in a light place maintaining a temperature of 50°F (10°C).
3. As the fresh green shoots appear, topdress the pot with further compost to leave a couple of inches of shoot standing proud of the compost's surface. Repeat until the pot is full.

Rhubarb crowns can be selected for forcing under greenhouse staging if not already done. Plunge them close together in a crate filled with moist peat, then cover with black polythene to encourage succulent pink shoots (right).

You need a lot of space to grow fruit successfully in a greenhouse. Vines, peaches, nectarines, apricots and figs all benefit from a heated environment, but they are so demanding that little else can be grown with them.

A high temperature of 61°F (16°C) is required if you want to start vines off in late winter, with a minimum night temperature of around 45°F (7°C) over the early spring period. A humid atmosphere must be maintained, which does not always fit in with other crops, and no ventilation should be given except on clear, still days. Feed and water well. Suitable varieties include 'Black Hamburg', 'Foster's Seedling' and 'Alicante'.

Pot-grown strawberry runners that were rooted during mid- and late summer should be brought inside and potted into 5in (12.5cm) containers. These plants need to be started into growth very gradually, raising the temperature slowly to about

10°C at night. When new growth appears, increase water rations. Several varieties are recommended including 'Idil' and 'Pantagruella'.

FEEDING, WATERING, HEAT AND AIR

Once chrysanthemums have finished flowering in the greenhouse and are carefully labelled cut back to about 6in (15cm) and carefully remove the debris. Light and air will then get down to the crown to encourage basal growths.

Charm chrysanthemums that have finished flowering need to be cut back. Keep them just moist in

Plunge rhubarb crowns in a crate of moist peat ...

... for succulent pink shoots in early spring

a frost-free position under the staging in the greenhouse or in a spare bedroom. Shoots will break from the stools during the next few weeks and make ideal material for cuttings if you wish to increase your stock for display next year.

Christmas cactus should be kept moist and fed once a week with a weak liquid fertilizer. Do not move the plant once it has budded up, otherwise you risk bud drop. Also keep it away from draughts, and give sufficient water to prevent too dry a compost, as neglect of either of these points will have the same effect.

Cyclamen will be flowering in early winter. They are particularly vulnerable to rot, so careful watering from below is a must. Regularly remove dying leaves and flowers by giving a sharp tug at the base of the stem.

Forced bulbs will need to be brought in from plunge beds if they are to be ready for mid-winter. Some folk like to sow grass seed around the bulbs to complete the decorative effect.

Feed pot plants like calceolarias, cinerarias and primulas with a high-potash fertilizer to encourage flowerbud production.

Clean up the greenhouse and scrape away at the loose flaky bark on the vine. Don't get carried away, but take it down to the smooth, brown bark under-

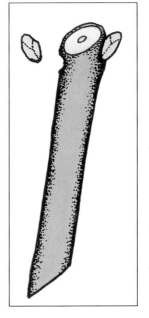

Eye cuttings are used for the fruiting Vitis vinifera *cultivars. They should be taken from woody one-year-old stems during winter. Remove one of the buds and dip base in hormone rooting powder. Insert in cuttings compost so that only the bud is showing. Water in and place in a propagator at 70°F (21° C). Top growth will occur before rooting takes place.*

neath. Take care not to damage the buds though. Removing the loose bark will reduce the pest and disease problems for next year by either spoiling their winter hide-aways or, more importantly, exposing those already hidden to an insecticide. Paint on an insecticide containing malathion for best results.

Remove the top inch or so of compost from the surface around fruit in the greenhouse and replace it with fresh loam. Dust on some sterilized bonemeal and sulphate of potash. Ventilate freely in order to keep temperatures down.

PINCHING OUT AND CUTTING BACK

Fuchsias grown as bushes will need pinching out a week or so after potting up from their 3½in (9cm) pots into 5in (12.5cm) containers.

Aechmea.

POLLINATION

During late winter, peaches, nectarines and apricots in a well-heated greenhouse start to come into flower. They are normally insect-pollinated but in the greenhouse this is a far from reliable method so some form of assistance must be given. (*See* the section on pollination in Chapter 6.)

Vines also need hand pollinating when they come into flower, which will be a month or so after they were started into growth.

Unheated greenhouses with vines should be well ventilated during the day to prevent plants shooting away too early and risking frost damage to the soft, young growth.

Some greenhouse climbers such as the passion flower (*Passiflora*) need to be cut back in midwinter if they're not to look straggly all season. Remove all weak and diseased shoots and prune back the current year's growth to a healthy, plump bud about 6in (15cm) from the main stem. Where the plant is becoming too big for the space available thin some shoots back to the main stem or even to ground level and cut others back as already described. Bougainvilleas, gardenias and pelargoniums need a trim after their winter rest. Cut back to about 6in (15cm) and repot with fresh compost.

OVERWINTERED FUCHSIAS

Overwintered fuchsias should be pruned back to produce a well-structured framework. Make each cut to an outward-facing bud ½in (1.25cm) or so from the main stem for standard types and to within 2in (5cm) of the crown for bush varieties.

Of course, all weak, tangled, diseased or dead growth must be completely removed.

CHAPTER 10

Pests and Diseases

DEALING WITH PESTS AND DISEASES

The greenhouse must seem like paradise to many pests and diseases – all that lush, green growth in a warm and inviting environment makes a veritable Garden of Eden. Lack of competition and perfect growing conditions are as much of an advantage to pests and diseases as to the plants being grown, so some form of protective measures must be taken to combat this ever-present threat of invasion.

Prevention is far better than cure when it comes to pests and diseases. This can be achieved to a large extent by simple hygiene, by keeping the greenhouse and its contents clean and tidy and removing any dead or dying plant material as soon as it is noticed before becoming infected.

Giving the greenhouse a thorough wash and brush-up during the less hectic winter months will reduce any carry-over problems from one season to the next. In addition, judicious watering and ventilation during the growing season will go a long way to preventing infection as well as restricting the spread of any pest or disease that has already gained a foothold.

During the growing season check all plants regularly for the first signs of pest and disease attack. If control measures are taken early, then fewer sprays of noxious chemicals will be necessary and little damage will have been caused.

PESTS

Ants

Identification Small brown social insects that form colonies.

PROBLEM PREVENTION

Many fruit problems are easy to prevent if you can maintain good growing conditions. Concentrate on getting the following:
✿ Provide sufficient shading and automatic ventilation to keep the greenhouse cool in summer and prevent temperature fluctuations.
✿ Provide sufficient water on a regular basis to prevent plants running short and becoming stressed.
✿ Provide the right food for steady and healthy growth. A high-potash tomato feed for fruit and flower crops and a balanced feed for other crops.

Crop Indiscriminate attackers of a range of pot-grown plants and crops in border soils.

Damage Their industrious nest-building activities can literally undermine root systems, causing the soil to become spongy. Furthermore, they farm aphids and scale insects like cattle so they can be 'milked' for their honeydew – a sugary substance these sap-sucking insects produce. Ants carry such pests onto unaffected plants to establish new colonies.

Treatment Infested pot-grown plants should be put into a bucket of water to soak overnight. Ant activities around the foundations and central pathways can be discouraged with boiling water. Alternatively, proprietary ant powders or poisonous baits can be laid down for the ants to carry back to their nest.

Aphids

Identification Small green and black sap-sucking insects more commonly known as greenfly or blackfly.

Crop Almost all plants are susceptible.

Damage Colonies of aphids will reduce plant growth rates through their sap-feeding activities and rapidly reproduce to overwhelm new growth. Aphids produce a sugary excretion called honeydew that is often colonized by a blanketing sooty mould fungus. They also transmit virus diseases from one plant to another.

Treatment Very small attacks early in the season can be washed off with soapy water. Consider applying a biological control (*see* Controlling Pests without Chemicals section). Routine chemical sprays may be necessary later in the season. Try to vary the chemical used so that this pest cannot build up a resistance. Most effective is to fumigate the greenhouse with a smoke cone containing an insecticide. Alternatively, spray with a contact or contact and systemic insecticide.

Caterpillars

Identification Long, soft-bodied grubs that are the larval stage of butterflies and moths.

Crop Different caterpillars attack various plants.

Damage They are avaricious consumers of leaves and sometimes fruits, producing large holes and depositing tell-tale black droppings. The carnation

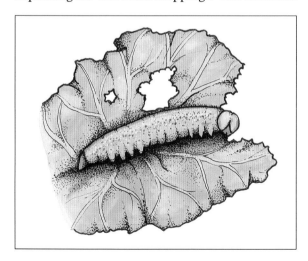

The small cabbage white caterpillar consumes leaves.

tortrix moth also produces webbing, holding leaves together. Flowerbuds may also be attacked.

Treatment Prevent adults entering the greenhouse by netting vents and the doorway. Individual grubs can be picked off by hand and disposed of. Consider applying a biological control (*see* Controlling Pests without chemicals section). For severe infestations, apply a contact or systemic insecticide.

Earwigs

Identification Very common medium-sized brown insect that has distinctive pincer-shaped tail.

Crop Mostly confined to ornamental shrubs like chrysanthemums, clematis, roses and dahlias.

Damage Usually found in dry spots where they attack and disfigure the blooms and young leaves. Their night-time forays result in ragged petals and leaves, making blooms unsightly.

Treatment Trap pests in inverted pots stuffed with newspaper or straw; matchboxes also prove effective. Each morning seal the traps, remove from the greenhouse and destroy them. Dust with a contact insecticide.

Eelworms

Identification Very thin, almost transparent, microscopic worms. They are difficult to see with the naked eye.

Crop Attack chrysanthemums, ferns, tomatoes and daffodils.

Damage Eelworms live inside the tissue where their rapid reproduction will cause loss of vigour. Chrysanthemum and fern eelworms cause lower leaves to yellow and go blotchy, eventually turning brown. On chrysanthemums small flowerbuds that develop are often disfigured. On other plants they cause leaves to distort and cysts to form on roots.

Treatment Remove and destroy badly affected plants. Dormant chrysanthemum stools can be

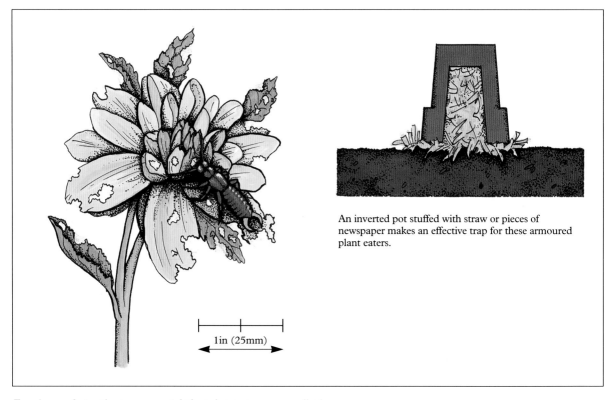

1in (25mm)

An inverted pot stuffed with straw or pieces of newspaper makes an effective trap for these armoured plant eaters.

Earwigs are destructive to ornamental plants but traps are very effective.

given hot water treatment (115°F; 46°C) – dipped for about five minutes. Sterilize infected soil or replace with fresh. Growing bags may be the answer to badly infected borders.

Fungus Flies (*Sciarids*)

Identification Tiny springing flies on and around compost that are just visible to the naked eye.

Crop Anywhere there is wet compost these flies thrive.

Damage The larval stage causes a little damage attacking roots, but it is not in any way serious and not worth controlling. Adults are annoying, though, so control is often sought.

Treatment Keep compost less wet; and you could try watering from beneath. Try yellow sticky traps. Very severe attacks can usually be successfully controlled with an insecticide.

Leafhopper

Identification Like aphids these pests are also sap-sucking, but jump away when disturbed.

Crop Attack a wide range of plants.

Damage Check the undersides of mottled leaves for the skin casts that they leave behind. They are rarely a real problem but, like aphids, can transmit viruses.

Treatment Remove badly affected leaves. Chemical control can be gained by spraying with a contact or contact and systemic insecticide.

Leaf Miner

Identification Minute pale green larvae of various species of fly; hatch from eggs laid just beneath the surface of the leaf. Easily identified by the damage they cause.

The leaf miner attacks exactly as its name suggests – the burrowing larvae weave intricate patterns just under the surface.

Crop Tomatoes, chrysanthemums, cinerarias and others.

Damage Intricate brown and creamy patterns on the leaf are caused by the burrowing larvae. This disfigures the leaf and in very severe attacks reduces vigour. Sometimes rather than rambling tunnels, small brown blisters can develop.

Treatment Control individual grubs by stabbing them with a pin or the point of a penknife. Otherwise cut off affected leaves and burn. Where a single plant is badly attacked remove and destroy it. Or spray with a systemic insecticide.

Leatherjackets

Identification Large greyish-brown soft-bodied grubs that live in the soil. They are the larvae of the cranefly or daddy-long-legs.

Crop This will attack anything grown in the border soil.

Damage This pest attacks the root system, causing plants to turn yellow and wilt. Severe attacks can kill the plants.

Treatment Mix in soil insecticide when the border is cultivated. Net vents to prevent adult craneflies entering the greenhouse in the first instance. Consider applying a biological control (*see* Controlling Pests without Chemicals section).

Mealy Bugs

Identification Small white, oval insects like miniature woodlice covered in a waxy woolly-looking secretion. They colonize leaf axils and leaf bases.

Crop Attack almost any permanent plant in the greenhouse, but particularly prevalent on vines, ferns, palms and figs.

Damage Again a sap-sucking insect that reduces vigour and exudes sticky honeydew, often colonized by debilitating sooty mould.

Treatment Isolated attacks can be treated with methylated spirit applied using a small paintbrush or swab of cotton wool. Treat severe attacks with systemic insecticide. Consider applying a biological control (*see* Controlling Pests without Chemicals section).

Millipedes

Identification A worm-like multi-legged creature that, unlike a centipede, has two legs per segment.

Crop Attacks many greenhouse plants, but particularly those with bulbs, tubers or corms.

Damage This pest usually feeds on decaying matter but will attack roots if food sources are in short supply. It also tunnels into bulbs and feeds on tubers and corms and usually enlarges initial attacks by other pests or diseases.

Treatment Clean up debris in the greenhouse. Pick up and destroy any millipedes found. Chemical control is not usually worth while.

Scale Insect

Identification Inconspicuous flat brown scales found on stems and leaves.

Crop Grapes, peaches, citrus, figs and many other greenhouse plants.

Damage Sap-sucking insects weaken the plant, reducing vigour. If left unchecked the sheer numbers will eventually kill the host. Honeydew excreted by these pests can cause a secondary infection of blanketing sooty mould fungus.

Treatment Isolated attacks can be treated with methylated spirit as with mealy bugs. For more severe infestations fortnightly sprays with a systemic insecticide will control immature stages of the pest's life cycle. Several treatments will be necessary.

Slugs

Identification A well-known soft-bodied pest. If not visible then look for the distinctive slime trail early in the day.

Crop A particular problem with seedlings of almost any crop as well as the soft green growth of more mature plants.

Damage Eat large holes in leaves, stems, shoots and roots.

Treatment Beer traps may work: bury a cup or a bowl up to its brim in the border soil and fill with beer. The beer-swilling pests are attracted to the edge and fall in the trap. Alternatively, scatter slug pellets around vulnerable plants.

Spider Mite

Identification Minute reddish-brown and fawn mites can be seen on the undersides of leaves. First signs of attack are usually the tiny white or yellow pin pricks on the upper surface that result from sap-sucking activity beneath. Webbing over leaves and stem are an easily recognizable sign of an established colony, but by this stage it is too late to control the pest.

Crop Tomatoes, cucumbers, carnations, vines, peaches, and many more greenhouse plants.

Slugs and snails are common garden pests: they eat soft green growth.

CONTROLLING PESTS WITHOUT CHEMICALS

If you don't want to use chemicals to control pests there are four basic non-chemical options: hand removed; barriers; traps; and using natural predators and parasites of the pest. The latter is often referred to as biological control.

By hand If a colony of insects such as aphids are spotted early enough, you can effectively control them by either squashing individual insects or washing them off with a jet of water. Picking off affected shoots is another option. With flying insects such as whiteflies, you could try sucking them up with a car vacuum cleaner.

Barriers Fine mesh netting on vents and doors will keep out flying insects and you can even use a non-drying glue barrier to prevent vine weevil attacks.

Traps Yellow sticky traps hung in the greenhouse will help control flying insects such as whitefly and fungus flies.

Biological controls Natural enemies of greenhouse pests that can be introduced to control the pest without using chemicals. Which biological control you choose depends on the pest you want to control.

HOW TO USE BIOLOGICAL CONTROLS

The main advantage of a biological control is that it is pest specific so that you know it will not attack any beneficial insects inside or outside the greenhouse. However, to use a biological control successfully you have to introduce them at the right time, give them the right conditions and not spray in the greenhouse while they are controlling the pest.

Biological controls are supplied by mail order. Even those on offer at garden centres are simply order forms for the biological control to be supplied by post. Biological controls do not arrive as adults but in a dormant stage. Some are dispatched attached to pieces of leaf or card, others arrive mixed with granules, while bacterium is supplied in sachets to be mixed with water and sprayed or watered on to the infested crop.

SIX STEPS FOR SUCCESS

1. Decide early in the season if you intend to use biological control and plan what you can and can't spray carefully.
2. Use a non-persistent chemical to control other pest problems before introducing the biological control.
3. Get the timing right. Order the biological control when you first see the pest attack.
4. Open the package containing the biological control immediately on arrival inside the greenhouse so that the biological control cannot escape.
5. Disperse the biological control evenly over the crop as directed by the supplier.
6. Do not spray once a biological control has been introduced. Wait until the pest is controlled and the biological control has largely died out.

WHICH BIOLOGICAL CONTROL?

pest	biological control
Aphid	predator (*Aphidoletes aphidimyza*) parasite (*Aphidius matricariae*)
Caterpillar	bacterium (*Bacillus thuringiensis*)
Leaf miner	parasite (*Dacnusa sibirica*)
Mealy bug	predator (*Cryptolaemus montrouzier*)
Scale insect	parasite (*Metaphycus helvolus*)
Sciarid fly	parasite (*Heterorhabditis*)
Spider mite	predator (*Phytoseiulus persimilis*)
Thrip	predator (*Amblyseius cucumeris*)
Vine weevil	parasite (*Heterorhabditis*)
Whitefly	parasite (*Encarsia formosa*)

Damage Leaves produce mottled effect, then yellow, causing loss of vigour. Eventually both leaves and blooms turn brown and die.

Treatment Since these pests thrive in warm, dry conditions, prevention is possible by encouraging a cooler, more humid, atmosphere. Spraying with chemicals has a limited effect, but a fortnightly treatment with an insecticide can help to control them. Try to vary the chemical used so that this pest cannot build up a resistance to the treatment over time.

Thrips

Identification These very small brown insects are commonly called thunder flies. When disturbed these pests move away quickly from the plant.

Crop Thrips are most prevalent on carnations and chrysanthemums, but they will also attack other plants.

Damage Often abundant in flowers and on leaves where they suck sap, causing mottling of leaves. Severe attacks result in disfigurement of petals and leaves as they develop.

Treatment Keep atmosphere moist to prevent this pest. Severe attacks can be controlled with systemic insecticide.

Tomato Moth

Identification Large green caterpillars 1½in (3.5cm) long feeding inside fruit.

Crop Tomatoes.

Damage Large holes in fruit, similar to that caused by slugs and snails. So, if no caterpillar present, look for tell-tale slime trails.

Treatment Remove affected fruit and any caterpillars or eggs found.

Vine Weevils

Identification Larvae white wrinkled C-shaped grubs about ½in (1.25cm) long with distinctive brown head.

Crop This pest will attack almost any pot plant as well as vines and peaches.

Damage The grubs eat roots, crowns, corms and tubers of primulas, begonias, cyclamen and many others. The adult will also attack the edges of leaves.

Treatment No chemical control. Consider applying a biological control (*see* Controlling Pests without Chemicals section).

Whitefly

Identification Small large-winged flies that can be found spreading rapidly on the undersides of leaves

An example of a vine weevil larva and adult.

of affected plants. They form large colonies that all fly up together in a white cloud when disturbed.

Crop Tomatoes, cucumbers, chrysanthemums, fuchsias and many more plants.

Damage As a sap-sucking insect it reduces vigour and yield of fruit crops. It must be dealt with very quickly because it has a tremendous rate of reproduction and so can soon cause serious problems. It also exudes honeydew that can be colonized by sooty mould.

Treatment Spray with systemic insecticide. Several sprays may be necessary to gain control. Consider applying a biological control (*see* Controlling Pests without Chemicals section).

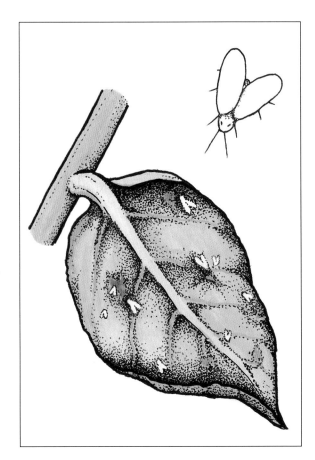

The sap-sucking whitefly.

Woodlice

Identification Grey-brown, hard-coated insects that look rather like miniature armadillos and thrive in cool, damp, shady spots.

Crop Cucumbers, tomatoes and some other crops.

Damage These pests feed at night nibbling at roots, stems and leaves. In severe cases plants can wilt and keel over.

Treatment Remove all debris from the greenhouse and a good programme of hygiene should eliminate them. Problem infestations can be controlled by dusting with an insecticide.

DISEASES

Anthracnose

Identification Pale green sunken spots on leaves and near the ends of the fruits.

Crop Cucumbers, melons.

Damage Encouraged by humid conditions, spots will eventually turn brown and enlarge until whole leaf withers and dies. Fruits turn yellow and die.

Treatment Regular sprays using a sulphur-based fungicide will help control this disease. Keep the greenhouse well ventilated. When the crop is removed at the end of the season sterilize the greenhouse thoroughly.

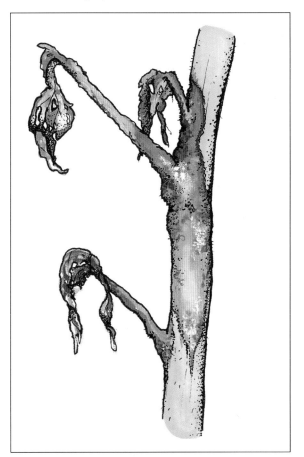

Botrytis or grey mould on tomato.

Botrytis

Identification A fluffy grey mould that will appear on leaves, stems, flowers and fruits. It is usually a secondary infection gaining a foothold on damaged tissues.

Crop Will attack a wide range of plants but the soft fleshy growth on cucumbers, tomatoes and melons is particularly vulnerable.

Damage As a secondary infection it develops most rapidly in cool, humid conditions where there is little or no ventilation. It gains entry through open wounds from pest attack, when fading flowers fall and by pruning or harvesting cuts. Infected plants will rot and die if left.

Treatment Good ventilation, generous air movement will stop the spread of the disease. Make sure you don't overcrowd the greenhouse, and pay particular attention to hygiene during the winter months when this disease is more difficult to cope with.

Remove diseased growth with a sharp knife and paint pruning wounds with a fungicide. Chemical control can be gained using systemic fungicide.

Blossom End Rot

Identification Brown, sunken, circular patches form on the blossom end of the developing fruits.

Crop Tomatoes, peppers.

Damage A fruit development disorder results from an induced calcium deficiency caused by insufficient or irregular watering.

Treatment Attention should be given to the feeding and watering programme for these crops.

Uneven Ripening

Identification Fruits ripen unevenly producing mottled colours of greens, reds and yellows.

Crop Tomatoes.

Blossom end rot.

Damage Renders affected fruit unappetising, caused by a nutrient deficiency in the compost. A shortage of nitrogen or potash is associated with high greenhouse temperatures.

Treatment Ventilation and a liquid feed will overcome this problem. The fruit is still edible.

Buckeye Rot

Identification Target-like brown concentric rings on surface of fruit.

Crop Tomatoes.

GROWING RESISTANT VARIETIES

If you have suffered from a disease problem regularly over recent years, one option is to grow a variety that is noted for showing some resistance. For instance the cucumber 'Mildana' has shown resistance to both downy and powdery mildew, while the aubergine 'Bonica' and the sweet pepper 'Bell Boy' offer resistance to tomato mosaic virus (TMV). There are a number of tomato varieties that exhibit resistance to TMV as well as leaf mould and wilt. Perhaps the best known is 'Shirley'.

Damage Soil-borne disease is splashed onto fruit during careless watering. Usually affecting lower trusses only.

Treatment Remove affected fruit. Watering carefully to avoid soil splash.

Dampening off

Identification A disease of seedlings in seedtrays or just after pricking out. Seedlings keel over with dark brown or black colouring at soil level. Sometimes small groups of seedlings topple in one area of a seedtray and sometimes several trays full of seeds succumb.

Splitting when ripening is caused by uneven watering.

Crop Almost any seedling.

Damage Basal rot of seedling stem causes it to keel over and die. Disease thrives in a humid atmosphere.

Treatment Prevention is the only answer. Use well-sterilized compost and seedtrays only. Sow seed thinly and keep developing seedlings well

ventilated. Where disease occurs water with 'Cheshunt Compound'.

Downy Mildew

Identification Yellow or brown patches (angular on cucumbers) on leaves which have corresponding white fungal tufts on the undersides.

Crop Cucumbers, melons, lettuce, cinerarias and seedlings.

Damage Disease particularly a problem in warm, moist conditions.

Treatment Remove affected leaves. Spray others with a systemic fungicide (not on cucumbers). Make sure greenhouse is well ventilated to keep humidity down.

Ghost Spotting

Identification Light, halo-like rings appear on the surface of the fruit.

Crop Tomatoes, peppers and aubergines.

Ghost spotting.

Leaf mould.

Damage Results from earlier unsuccessful attack by botrytis or grey mould fungus. The halo effect is produced as the fruit grows and expands.

Treatment No chemical treatment, but prevent problems in future by discouraging botrytis.

Leaf Mould

Identification Undersides of lower leaves have purplish-brown areas and upper leaf surfaces may develop yellow patches.

Crop Tomatoes, peppers and aubergines.

Damage Lower leaves attacked especially in warm and humid conditions.

Treatment Spray with a systemic fungicide regularly and ventilate greenhouse well. It is worth watering plants at the beginning of the day rather than the end. Grow resistant varieties.

Potato Blight

Identification Large, dark brown patches on leaves, stems and fruit.

Crop Potatoes, tomatoes.

Damage Spots increase in size and number to cover, whole leaf and eventually whole plants cease to grow.

Treatment There is no chemical control. Preventative sprays of copper-based fungicides can be tried. Otherwise, remove and destroy affected plants. Also spray any other potato crops nearby.

Powdery Mildew

Identification White dusting on youngest shoots and leaves. Edges of leaves may curl under.

Crop Not fussy what greenhouse plants it attacks.

Damage Affected tissues will eventually turn yellow and shrivel. Most prevalent in hot, dry seasons.

Powdery mildew.

WHAT'S WRONG?

Symptom	Cause	Solution
Tomato fruit		
Bronzing when green, corky flesh	Tobacco mosaic virus	Remove affected fruit. Practice good greenhouse hygiene. Choose resistant varieties.
Brown concentric rings	Buckeye rot	Remove affected fruit. Take care not to splash soil onto fruits when watering.
Dark areas on bottom of fruit	Blossom end rot	Remove affected fruit. Water regularly especially in hot weather.
Fruits eaten	Tomato moth	Remove affected fruit, caterpillars and any eggs found.
Hollow fruit	Irregular watering or potassium deficiency or weedkiller damage	Feed with high-potash tomato feed. Water regularly in hot weather.
Pale brown patches	Sun scald	Shade and ventilate greenhouse well, especially in hot weather.
Poor setting	Irregular watering or dry atmosphere	Keep humidity high by damping down. Shake flower trusses daily.
Rotten with fluffy appearance	Grey mould (*Botrytis*)	Remove affected fruit. Practise good greenhouse hygiene and keep humidity down.
Small grey spots or rings	Ghost spotting	Practise good greenhouse hygiene and keep humidity down.
Small fruit	Poor pollination or dry atmosphere	Keep humidity high by damping down. Shake flower trusses daily.
Splitting when ripening	Irregular watering	Water regularly especially in hot weather.
Yellow patches on shoulder	Greenback	Shade and ventilate greenhouse. Feed with high-potash tomato feed.
Uneven ripening	Potash deficiency or too much heat	Feed with high-potash tomato feed. Water regularly and ventilate well in hot weather.
Tomato leaves		
Brown edges	Potato blight	Apply a copper-based fungicide. Destroy badly affected plants.
Clouds of white insects	Whitefly	Apply a contact insecticide every three days. Or try yellow sticky traps, car vacuum cleaner or a biological control.
Green insects, sticky leaves	Aphids	Apply systemic insecticide or use a biological control.

WHAT'S WRONG?

Symptom	Cause	Solution
Powdery black spots, sticky leaves	Sooty mould	Wash with soapy water. Control sap-sucking insects such as aphids.
Rolled mature leaves	Temperature changes	None necessary.
Stems and leaves distorted	Weedkiller damage	Destroy badly affected plants. Take care when spraying near greenhouse.
Speckled yellow, turning brown	Spider mite	Remove badly affected shoots. Keep humidity high. Apply systemic insecticide or use a biological control.
Wilt and turn yellow	Wilt disease	Keep greenhouse warm and water carefully. Use growing bags.
Yellow between the veins	Magnesium deficiency	Apply Epsom salts (magnesium sulphate) to affected plants.
Yellow, mottled and distorted	Viruses	Remove affected plants. Control sap-sucking insects such as aphids.
Yellow patches, brown underneath	Leaf mould	Apply a systemic fungicide regularly. Shade and ventilate to lower humidity and control temperatures.

Cucumber fruit

Symptom	Cause	Solution
Bitter fruits	Pollination	Remove male flowers (those without swelling at base of flower). Grow a modern all-female variety.
Grey oozing spots	Gummosis	Remove affected fruit. Next time, raise greenhouse temperatures and ventilate well in hot weather.
Pale green sunken spots	Anthracnose	Apply a sulphur-based fungicide regularly. Ventilate well. Practise good hygiene.
Wither and die when young	Withering	Remove affected fruits. Apply a foliar feed. Water carefully.

Cucumber leaves

Symptom	Cause	Solution
Brown edges	Temperature too high	Shade and ventilate the greenhouse well, especially in hot weather.
Clouds of white insects	Whitefly	Apply a contact insecticide every three days. Or try yellow sticky traps, car vacuum cleaner or a biological control.
Green insects, sticky leaves	Aphids	Apply systemic insecticide or use a biological control.

WHAT'S WRONG?

Symptom	Cause	Solution
Lower leaves yellow and wilt	Wilt disease	Keep greenhouse warm and water carefully. Use growing bags.
Mottled and distorted	Cucumber mosaic virus (CMV)	Remove affected plants. Control sap-sucking insects such as aphids.
Pale green sunken spots	Anthracnose	Apply a sulphur-based fungicide regularly. Ventilate well. Practise good hygiene.
Speckled yellow, turning brown	Spider mite	Remove badly affected shoots. Keep humidity high. Apply systemic insecticide or use a biological control.
White powdery coating	Powdery mildew	Apply a systemic fungicide regularly. Ventilate and water well in hot weather.
Yellow angular spots, downy tufts underneath	Downy mildew	Ventilate and water well in hot weather.

Pepper fruit

Symptom	Cause	Solution
Dark areas on bottom of fruit	Blossom end rot	Remove affected fruit. Water regularly, especially in hot weather.
Rot with fluffy appearance	Grey mould (*Botrytis*)	Remove affected fruit. Practise good greenhouse hygiene and keep humidity down.

Pepper leaves

Symptom	Cause	Solution
Clouds of white insects	Whitefly	Apply a contact insecticide every three days. Or try yellow sticky traps, car vacuum cleaner or a biological control.
Green insects, sticky leaves	Aphids	Apply systemic insecticide or use a biological control.
Speckled yellow, turning brown	Spider mite	Remove badly affected shoots. Keep humidity high. Apply systemic insecticide or use a biological control.
Yellow, mottled and distorted	Viruses	Remove affected plants. Control sap-sucking insects such as aphids.

Lettuce leaves

Symptom	Cause	Solution
Green insects, sticky leaves	Aphids	Apply systemic insecticide or use a biological control.
Mottled yellow, white undersides	Downy mildew	Remove affected leaves. Apply a systemic fungicide and ventilate well.
No heart	Lack of light or nutrients	Space 12in (30cm) apart. Feed and water regularly.

WHAT'S WRONG?		
Symptom	**Cause**	**Solution**
Rotten with fluffy appearance	Grey mould (*Botrytis*)	Remove affected fruit. Practise good greenhouse hygiene and keep humidity down.
Run to seed (bolt)	Check in growth	Avoid checks in growth when planting. Keep well watered.
Scorched edges	Irregular watering	Water well, especially in hot weather.

Treatment Keep air circulating and the temperature down by means of careful ventilation, with frequent damping down to increase humidity, but avoid wetting the plants. Remove badly affected leaves. Spray regularly with a systemic fungicide immediately first signs of attack are noticed.

Rust

Identification Tiny orange-brown pinhead spots form on the undersides of the leaves and release a cloud of spores when disturbed.

Crop Can affect pelargoniums, fuchsias, carnations, chrysanthemums and others.

Damage Not a common problem, but if it occurs rust can have a disastrous effect on crops.

Treatment Improve air circulation, avoid high-nitrogen fertilizers, and practise good greenhouse hygiene. Destroy badly infected plants, then spray others with a systemic fungicide and repeat at 10–14 day intervals.

Sooty Mould

Identification Leaves and fruit covered in sooty black mould.

Crop Any plants attacked by sap-sucking insects.

Damage Black sooty mould grows on the sugary honeydew excreted by sap-sucking insects. In severe cases black coating can inhibit photosynthesis.

Treatment Wash off with soapy water and control sap-sucking insects such as aphids.

Viruses

Identification Various forms of leaf distortion, yellowing and mottling result from infection. More than one virus may infect a plant at the same time.

Crop A range of greenhouse plants are susceptible.

Damage Growth becomes weakened with an associated loss of vigour. Distortion of leaves can make plants unattractive and produce misshapen flowers.

Treatment Root out all affected plants. The control of sap-sucking insects that spread viruses is the only effective way of keeping your greenhouse free.

Wilt

Identification Wilting of lower leaves during the day (they often recover at night) is the first sign.

Crop Carnations and tomatoes.

Damage Recovery of wilting leaves is only temporary. They eventually discolour and drop – starting at the base and slowly progressing up the plant.

Treatment Remove and destroy the affected plants. Sterilize the soil thoroughly before the next crop. Choose wilt-resistant varieties when replanting tomatoes. Best of all, change to growing in bags or containers.

Index